appetizers

appetizers
easy and delicious

Marisa Curatolo

Whitecap Books
Vancouver/Toronto

Edited by Elaine Jones
Proofread by Elizabeth McLean
Design by Antonia Banyard
Typesetting by Warren Clark
Cover and interior photographs by Lionel Trudel
Food styling by Nathan Fong

Printed and bound in Canada by Friesens, Altona, Manitoba.

Canadian Cataloguing in Publication Data

Curatolo, Marisa
    Appetizers

    Includes index
    ISBN 1-55110-859-3

    1. Appetizers. I. Title.
TX740.C87 1999   641.8'12   C98-911016-8

The publisher acknowledges the support of the Canada Council for the Arts and the Cultural Services Branch of the Government of British Columbia for our publishing program. We acknowledge the financial support of the Government of Canada through the Book Industry Development Program for our publishing activities.

*For my husband Michael
and sons Evan and Nicholas*

Contents

Casual Entertaining

Acknowledgments

To my loving husband Michael, for his endless support, humor and patience in the creation of this book. Hugs and kisses to my sweet little sons, Evan and Nicholas.

Thanks to my wonderful parents, Rosaria and Rocky, for their constant help during the writing of my book.

Thank you to my mother-in-law Wendy MacDonald for the late night readings of the manuscript and for giving me inspiration and guidance.

A warm thanks to my students at The Cooking Studio for their constant feedback on what they like to cook and eat.

Introduction

The way we entertain has changed dramatically over the years. I have fond memories of my mother and grandmother spending days in the kitchen preparing for a party. They would begin by making homemade preserves, baking breads and making pastry. As the day of the party approached, the tempo would pick up. Finishing touches would be made to the menu and the serving tables prepared. When party day arrived, there was the magic of setting elegant tables laden with fragrant food and the joyous sense of fun and camaraderie as the guests gathered together around a tantalizing banquet. Those warm childhood memories of the excitement and the anticipation of entertaining have inspired my love of cooking and remain with me today.

Today's cooks rarely have the luxury of spending this much time on a party. Busy lives and hectic schedules dictate recipes that can be made simply and stored until the day of the party. The purpose of this book is to encourage you to enjoy entertaining at home, whether you are planning a casual get-together with friends or an elegant black-tie affair. Here you will find practical tips for planning menus, organizing shopping lists and preparing food in advance, as well as suggestions for effortless table presentation, colorful garnishes and safe food storage. The recipes are both delicious and easy to prepare. They are perfect for the novice cook who finds the task of entertaining daunting and would rather call a caterer. Experienced cooks will love the simplicity and the range and variety of menu choices.

Some of the recipes are updated versions of classic and ethnic recipes from around the world; others are old party standbys, such as spinach dip or sausage puffs. You'll find many low-fat versions of familiar recipes (for example, hummus can be prepared with whole sesame seed as a substitute for high-fat ground sesame paste) and tips for eliminating fat in many dips and spreads by substituting fat-free sour cream, low-fat mayonnaise or yogurt cheese. Many recipes suggest the purchase of store-bought sauces and pastry dough as a time-saving strategy: the busy cook can now purchase precleaned shrimp, frozen bread dough and bottled salsa, for instance.

The recipes here offer a wide range of choices, from vegetarian to meat-based, simple to elaborate, casual to elegant. To make it easier to identify recipes with no meat, poultry or fish, all vegetarian recipes are marked with a 🚲. (They may contain eggs or dairy products.) The serving suggestions are designed to encourage you to experiment with ingredients, so use your imagination and have fun creating your own unique versions of these tried and true appetizers.

Menu Planning

Before you plan your menu, you need to decide on the appropriate style to suit the occasion. Will your gathering be formal or informal, large or small, daytime or evening, a casual get-together, or an elegant affair? Before you draw up your shopping list, consider the following points.

- Be sensitive to the dietary needs of your guests, their preferences and dislikes.
- Be aware of availability of ingredients due to seasonal variations.
- Plan dishes that are not repetitive in terms of color, seasoning and ingredients (for instance, chicken salad as well as a chicken main dish). Dishes should be complementary and appetizers should be different shapes.
- Choose dishes that are quick and easy to prepare, especially if you are the only one in the kitchen.
- Enlist the help of a friend or hire a helper to serve guests so you can spend time socializing.
- Choose finger foods that can be prepared in advance and frozen (there are many such recipes in this book, such as Beef and Tomato Empanadas or Wild Mushroom Turnovers).
- Serve dips and spreads with store-bought crackers and breads.
- Mix your recipe choices. Serve simple dishes with fancy, exotic items and balance heavy, rich dishes with low-fat choices; this makes for an interesting presentation that will appeal to every one of your guests.
- Plan a menu that is not too time-consuming. If you exhaust yourself, you may never feel like entertaining again.

Food Quantity Planning

The quantity of food to serve at your party will depend on the time and the purpose of the function. For example, a before-dinner cocktail party requires 6 to 8 hors d'oeuvres per guest, from a selection of 2 or 3 choices. Prepare items that are not too filling or elaborate. For an evening cocktail reception, a good rule of thumb is to offer 12 to 16 pieces per guest, from 5 or 6 choices. Too many choices will make it difficult for guests to appreciate your different menu selections.

Provide more substantial foods, such as meatballs, chicken sauté, or grilled Italian sausage, especially when drinks will be consumed. Include a vegetable platter and several dips and spreads. For a large group, food should be bite-size and easy to handle with one hand while juggling a glass of wine or a drink. Smaller groups that will gather around a coffee table or dining room table can be offered a fork and foods that are more difficult to handle. Try not to serve dishes with messy sauces that will drip and cause damage to clothing or furniture.

Presentation Ideas

Arrange each type of hors d'oeuvre individually on a small serving platter. This allows the guest time to choose an item and the display will look simple and enticing. Avoid crowding the platter with too many pieces and leave enough space for a sprig of herbs or a flower blossom. Platters look unfinished when time has not been taken to add a pretty garnish. Platters and baskets can be garnished with bouquets of fresh herbs, blossoms or unusual lettuce leaves; experiment with kale, spinach, chicory or lemon and lime wedges. Parsley works well as a bed for finger foods that might roll around when being passed, such as stuffed eggs or cherry tomatoes. Remember that fried food will become soggy if placed on a bed of greens.

To enhance the attractiveness of your presentation, line silver platters or plates with paper doilies. A simple and quick idea is to dust white plates with paprika and sprinkle finely chopped parsley or edible flower petals over the food. Before the party choose the serving dishes for your hor d'oeuvres.

Wicker baskets can hold chips and attractive ceramic bowls work well for dips and nuts, but let your imagination run free when it comes to serving hors d'oeuvres—try a piece of tile or granite, a wooden cutting board, a small mirror or clear or colored glass blocks.

Walk around your house and decide where foods should be placed. Avoid placing all the platters on the dining room table as guests will cluster around and make the table area very crowded. If possible, set up the bar in another room or on a separate table or counter to avoid overcrowding.

For large parties, pass foods on large platters to ensure that everyone is served and prevent too many people from gathering around the main dining table. For a smaller gathering, place food on a coffee table to facilitate conversation and create a cozy environment. Remember to place candles strategically around the room and dim the lights. Platters should be replenished when they are half empty. You can prepare two sets of hors d'oeuvres ahead of time and keep one in the kitchen. Provide small plates and plenty of napkins and toothpicks. I like to place small baskets lined with napkins around the room, so guests may dispose of skewers, shrimp tails, soiled napkins or bones.

Organization

It's very important to plan your party ahead of time. Shopping and task lists will eliminate running to the store several times. Check your pantry for items you already have on hand. Check recipes to make items that can be frozen in advance.

Set up the bar and arrange your table and flowers the day before. Cut and store vegetables a day in advance in reusable bags, which are easy to stack in the refrigerator. Some dips and spreads in the following chapters develop more flavor when they have a chance to sit prior to the function.

Freezing Food

Freezing food allows you to do some preparation in advance, and enables you to entertain unexpected guests without panicking. Freeze food in the uncooked stage and allow extra cooking time. The best way to freeze pastry such as turnovers, bouchée, empanadas or phyllo triangles is to line a baking sheet with parchment paper or waxed paper, arrange the pastry in a single layer and place the trays in the freezer. When they are frozen solid, carefully place them in an airtight container or freezer bags. To cook them, place the frozen hors d'oeuvres on a baking sheet and bake in a preheated oven for 10 minutes longer than the recipe specifies.

Freeze finger foods no longer than 3 to 6 months ahead of time and label them with the type of food and date of preparation. Make sure to wrap foods properly to prevent them from drying out and developing a freezer taste. Airtight containers and freezer bags work well for fragile foods. Just remember to squeeze out the excess air to prevent freezer burn.

Some Sample Menus

A Cocktail Party

Stilton Walnut Spread
Smoked Salmon Sushi Roll
Southwestern Crab Cakes
Parmesan Palmiers
Spiced Pecans

Al Fresco Reception

Baba Ghanoush
Tuna Caper Pâté
Red Pepper and Pesto Tortilla Rolls
Grilled Garlic Shrimp
Curried Chicken Bouchées

A Bridal Shower

Warm Artichoke and Goat Cheese Spread
Wild Mushroom Turnovers
Pâté à Choux with Chicken Almond Salad
Cucumber Rounds with Smoked Salmon Mousse
Roast Beef and Chive Butter Canapés

A Tailgate Party

Chorizo con Queso Dip
Honey-Glazed Meatballs
Buffalo Chicken Wings
Crispy Potato Skins
Tomato Basil Bruschetta
Chinese Wontons

Mediterranean Party

Marinated Lemon Olives
Hummus
Polenta Squares with Roasted Red Pepper Sauce
Moroccan Beef Kebabs
Rosemary and Onion Foccacia

Dips and Spreads

This chapter contains an array of dips and spreads from all over the world—zesty French provençal Tapenade, spicy Mexican Salsa Cruda, Middle Eastern Baba Ghanoush, Greek Tzatziki and many more.

Use these quick and easy recipes when unexpected guests drop by. You can whip most of them up in minutes, or prepare them in advance and store them in airtight containers in the refrigerator for days before you entertain.

Use crackers, breadsticks, potato chips, tortilla chips, shrimp and rice crackers, pita bread or pumpernickel and other breads to scoop up dips. They are equally good as a base for canapés.

Be creative with your presentation. Spread creamy dips into hollowed-out red bell peppers, baby pumpkins, miniature squashes, large firm tomatoes or halved pineapple. Hollow out rounds of crusty bread to form an edible bowl filled with creamy spinach or hot crab dip. Garnish with fresh edible flowers or slices of lemon and lime, sprigs of dill or fresh snipped chives to add color and beauty to your table.

Warm Artichoke and Goat Cheese Spread

Makes 3 cups (720 mL)

1	19-oz (540-mL) can artichoke hearts, drained and finely chopped	1
1	clove garlic, minced	1
2 Tbsp.	chopped fresh parsley	30 mL
1 Tbsp.	prepared horseradish	15 mL
1 cup	sour cream	240 mL
1 cup	mayonnaise	240 mL
6 oz.	mild goat cheese	170 g
1/4 cup	grated Parmesan cheese	60 mL
2 Tbsp.	slivered almonds	30 mL

Preheat the oven to 350ºF (175ºC).

Combine the artichoke hearts, garlic, parsley, horseradish, sour cream and mayonnaise. Beat in the goat cheese and Parmesan cheese.

Transfer to a medium baking dish. Bake for 20 minutes, until bubbly and heated through. Sprinkle with almonds and serve immediately. The dip can be stored, covered, in the refrigerator for two days. Bake just before serving.

Serve this creamy, warm spread with Pumpernickel Toast Points (page 164), grilled French bread and assorted vegetables. Leftover spread can be used to flavor mashed potatoes or as a fabulous sandwich filling with chopped tomatoes, alfalfa sprouts and cucumbers. To reduce the fat in this recipe, use a light sour cream or mayonnaise.

Tapenade

Makes 1 1/2 cups (360 ml)

Tapenade is the most popular appetizer in Provence. There are dozens of variations, but all contain ripe olives and fragrant garlic. Serve this spread with freshly toasted French bread or with an assortment of raw vegetables.

1 cup	black olives (kalamata or niçoise), rinsed, pitted and finely chopped	240 mL
2 Tbsp.	capers, rinsed and finely chopped	30 mL
2	cloves garlic, minced	2
2 Tbsp.	fresh lemon juice	30 mL
2 Tbsp.	extra-virgin olive oil	30 mL
1 Tbsp.	chopped fresh thyme, or 1/2 tsp. (2.5 mL) dried	15 mL
1/2 cup	chopped fresh parsley	120 mL
	salt to taste	
1/2 tsp.	freshly ground black pepper	2.5 mL
1 tsp.	lemon zest (optional)	5 mL

Combine the olives, capers, garlic, lemon juice, olive oil, thyme and parsley in a food processor or blender. Process only until the mixture is coarsely ground. Do not overprocess into a paste. Season with salt and pepper.

Transfer to a small serving bowl. Sprinkle with the lemon zest if desired. Let stand at room temperature for 1 hour before serving to allow the flavors to blend. The spread can be stored in an airtight container in the refrigerator for 1 week.

Tzatziki

Makes 2 cups (475 mL)

1/2	medium English cucumber	1/2	
2	cloves garlic, finely minced	2	
2 Tbsp.	chopped fresh mint	30 mL	
2 Tbsp.	fresh lemon juice	30 mL	
1/4 tsp.	cayenne pepper	1.2 mL	
1	small tomato, seeded and diced	1	
1 1/2 cups	Yogurt Cheese (page 167)	360 mL	
	salt and freshly ground black pepper to taste		
	fresh mint leaves (optional)		

This classic Middle Eastern cucumber and yogurt dip is traditionally served with wedges of fresh pita bread. I like to serve this cool dip with crispy fried food and spicy meat dishes.

Finely grate the cucumbers into a coffee filter or cheesecloth. Gather up the sides with your hands and gently squeeze out the liquid. This will prevent the sauce from thinning out.

Combine the cucumber, garlic, mint, lemon juice, cayenne and tomato. Add the yogurt cheese and beat until smooth. Season with salt and pepper. Transfer to a serving bowl and garnish with mint leaves if desired. Serve chilled or at room temperature. The dip can be stored in an airtight container in the refrigerator for 3 days.

Hummus

Makes 1 1/2 cups (360 mL)

This is a lighter version of the traditional Middle Eastern dish. Tahini—ground sesame paste—has been replaced with whole sesame seeds and pesto sauce. Use a store-bought pesto if you don't have homemade on hand. The secret to a non-fat creamy spread is to omit rinsing the chickpeas. I like to spoon the hummus mixture into an acorn squash cut in half. Serve with wedges of pita bread that have been lightly toasted in the oven.

1	19-oz. (540-mL) can chickpeas, drained	1
3	cloves garlic, minced	3
2 Tbsp.	fresh lemon juice	30 mL
2 Tbsp.	sesame seeds, toasted	30 mL
1 tsp.	Pesto (see page 168)	5 mL
2 Tbsp.	olive oil	30 mL
2 Tbsp.	chopped fresh parsley	30 mL
1/4 tsp.	freshly ground black pepper	1.2 mL
2 Tbsp.	chopped fresh cilantro (optional)	30 mL

In a food processor, combine the chickpeas, garlic, lemon juice, sesame seeds and pesto. Pulse several times until the mixture is coarsely chopped. Add the olive oil, parsley and pepper. Purée until smooth and creamy. Transfer the mixture to a serving bowl and sprinkle with cilantro if desired. Serve at room temperature.

The dip can be stored in an airtight container in the refrigerator for up to 1 week.

Guacamole

Makes 1 1/2 cups (360 mL)

2	large ripe avocados	2
1	clove garlic, minced	1
1/4 cup	finely diced red onion	60 mL
1	jalapeño chili, seeded and finely chopped	1
1/4 cup	chopped fresh cilantro	60 mL
1/4 cup	fresh lime juice	60 mL
	salt and freshly ground black pepper to taste	

Cut the avocados in half. Remove and discard the pits. Scoop the flesh from the skin into a medium bowl and mash the avocado with a fork. Mix in the garlic, onion, jalapeño chili, cilantro and lime juice to form a chunky spread. Season with salt and pepper. Transfer to a serving bowl. Cover and refrigerate until ready to serve.

The dip can be covered and kept in the refrigerator for up to 4 hours. Bring it back to room temperature before serving.

Guacamole is often served in Mexico as a garnish for tacos and in a creamy dip with homemade tortilla chips and assorted vegetables. Look for the black-skinned Hass avocados, which have bumpy, wrinkled skin and creamy flesh. To speed up the ripening process, place avocados in a brown bag with a banana at room temperature. Keep ripe avocados in the refrigerator. To prevent cut avocados from turning brown when exposed to air, rub the exposed flesh with lemon juice or wrap in plastic wrap.

 # Caponata

Makes 6 cups (1.5 L)

Caponata is a Sicilian vegetable ratatouille, in which the vegetables are cooked separately and then flavored with fresh herbs. The following version is quicker and allows you to cook everything in the same pan. Serve it with crusty bread or raw vegetables, or spoon it over grilled fish. I like to use purple, thin-skinned Japanese eggplant if it's available. It has a sweet, non-bitter flavor and does not need to be salted.

2	medium eggplants	2
1/3 cup	olive oil	80 mL
2 Tbsp.	olive oil	30 mL
1	large onion, chopped	1
3	cloves garlic, minced	3
4	celery stalks, diced	4
2	large red bell peppers, chopped	2
3	tomatoes, seeded and chopped	3
1/2 cup	pitted and chopped black kalamata olives	120 mL
1/4 cup	red wine vinegar	60 mL
	salt and freshly ground black pepper to taste	
1/2 cup	chopped fresh parsley	120 mL

Cut the eggplant into 1/2-inch (1-cm) cubes. If you are not using Japanese eggplants, place the cubes in a colander and sprinkle with salt. Let it sit for 10 minutes to allow the bitter juices to be drawn out. Pat it dry.

In a large non-stick frying pan, heat the 1/3 cup (80 mL) olive oil over medium-high heat. Add the eggplant and cook until brown and tender. Remove with a slotted spoon and drain on paper towels. Add the 2 Tbsp. (30 mL) olive oil and heat. Add the onion and garlic and cook about 6 minutes, or until tender and fragrant. Add the celery and red pepper. Cook for several minutes. Add the tomatoes and olives, and bring to a boil. Return the eggplant to the pan. Reduce the heat and cook gently for 10 minutes.

Add the red wine vinegar, salt and pepper. Stir in the parsley. Cool to room temperature before transferring to a serving dish.

The dip can be stored in an airtight container in the refrigerator for 4 days and brought back to room temperature before serving.

Chorizo con Queso Dip

Makes approximately 2 cups (475 mL)

1/2 lb.	chorizo or pork sausage, casing removed, minced	225 g
1	small onion, minced	1
1/2 cup	tomato juice	120 mL
1	4-oz. (113-mL) can chopped green chilies, drained	1
1 lb.	grated Monterey Jack cheese, about 4 cups (950 mL)	455 g
2 Tbsp.	finely chopped green onions	30 mL

Serve this spicy, tangy dip with chilled Mexican beer and crisp tortilla chips. Chorizo is a spicy Mexican sausage made from pork and seasoned with chilies, garlic and cumin. Look for it in the deli section of your local supermarket.

In a large non-stick frying pan, cook the chorizo over medium heat until pink (chorizo will turn pink when cooked). Add the onion and cook until soft and fragrant. Add the tomato juice, chilies and cheese. Cook until the cheese is thoroughly melted. Transfer to a serving dish and sprinkle with the green onions. Serve warm.

The dip can be stored in a covered container in the refrigerator for 3 days and warmed before serving.

Sun-Dried Tomato Cream Cheese Spread

This easy, delicious spread can be served with crusty baguettes, water crackers or crostini. Or try piping the filling into hollowed-out cherry tomatoes, blanched snow peas or crispy pastry puffs. For an attractive serving dish, place the spread in a large, hollowed-out red bell pepper and garnish with fresh basil leaves. Light cream cheese or Yogurt Cheese (page 167) can be used in place of regular cream cheese.

Makes 1 cup (240 ml)

6	dry-packed sun-dried tomatoes	6
1	8-oz. (225-g) package cream cheese, softened	1
2 oz.	Brie cheese, rind removed	60 g
2 Tbsp.	chopped fresh basil, or 1/2 tsp. (2.5 mL) dried basil	30 mL
2 Tbsp.	extra-virgin olive oil	30 mL
1/4 tsp.	freshly ground black pepper	1.2 mL
1/4 tsp.	salt	1.2 mL
	fresh basil leaves (optional)	

Place the tomatoes in a small bowl and add hot water to cover. Soak about 15 minutes, until the tomatoes are soft. Drain the tomatoes, discarding the liquid.

Combine the cream cheese, Brie and sun-dried tomatoes in a food processor or blender. Process until the mixture is smooth. Add chopped basil, olive oil, pepper and salt and whip until fluffy. Place in a serving bowl and garnish with basil leaves if desired. Serve at room temperature.

The spread can be covered and stored in the refrigerator for 2 weeks. Bring it back to room temperature before serving.

Facing page (clockwise from top): *Tapenade (p. 12), Hummus (p. 14), and Tzatziki (p. 13)*.

Following page: *Cheddar Cheese Ball (p. 27), Stilton Walnut Spread (p. 28), and Pita Chips (p. 166)*.

Pesto Dip

Makes ³/4 cup (180 mL)

¹/4 cup	Pesto (page 168)	60 mL
1 tsp.	fresh lemon juice	5 mL
¹/2 cup	mayonnaise	120 mL
¹/4 tsp.	salt	1.2 mL
¹/8 tsp.	freshly ground black pepper	.5 mL
1 Tbsp.	toasted pine nuts (optional)	15 mL

Combine the pesto, lemon juice and mayonnaise. Season with salt and pepper. Transfer to a serving bowl and sprinkle with the pine nuts if desired. Cover and chill.

The dip can be stored in an airtight container in the refrigerator for 5 days.

A wonderful, fresh-tasting dipping sauce for assorted crudités. A prepared pesto sauce can be used and is available in most supermarkets. To reduce the amount of fat in the recipe, use a light or a fat-free mayonnaise.

Toasting Nuts

There are three quick methods for toasting nuts. A dry skillet is excellent for pine nuts because they have a high fat content and burn quickly. To use the oven method, spread the nuts on a baking sheet and roast for 5–10 minutes at 350⁰F (175⁰C), turning often. Use a timer so you don't become distracted and let them burn.

To use the microwave, place up to ¹/2 cup (120 mL) nuts in a dish and microwave for 60 seconds on high.

Salsa Cruda

Makes 1 cup (240 mL)

This fresh tomato salsa is full of flavor, with just the right degree of spiciness. Serve it with Rainbow Tortilla Chips (page 165), spoon it over grilled fish or chicken, or mix it into scrambled eggs.

4	small tomatoes, seeded and diced	4
2 Tbsp.	finely sliced green onion	30 mL
1/2 cup	finely chopped fresh cilantro	120 mL
1	jalapeño, seeded and finely chopped	1
1 Tbsp.	red wine vinegar	15 mL
1 Tbsp.	fresh lemon juice	15 mL
2 Tbsp.	vegetable oil	30 mL
	salt and freshly ground black pepper to taste	
	lemon slices (optional)	

Combine the tomatoes, green onion, cilantro and jalapeño in a non-reactive bowl. Add the vinegar, lemon juice and oil. Mix well. Season with salt and pepper. Garnish with lemon slices if desired. Let stand at room temperature for 30 minutes before serving to allow the flavors to blend.

The salsa can be stored in an airtight container in the refrigerator for 1 day.

Cilantro

Fresh cilantro is also sold as Chinese parsley or coriander. It is a popular herb in Middle Eastern, Asian and Mexican cooking. The leaves can be chopped and added to almost any dish. Look for it in the produce department of your local supermarket. To store it, place the roots in a glass of cold water and cover the leaves loosely with plastic wrap. It will keep for about 1 week in the refrigerator.

Roasted Red Pepper Sauce

Makes 1½ cups (360 mL)

½ cup	mayonnaise	120 mL
½ cup	sour cream	120 mL
2 Tbsp.	fresh lemon juice	30 mL
1 Tbsp.	chopped fresh parsley	15 mL
¼ cup	roasted red peppers (see page 67)	60 mL
¼ tsp.	salt	1.2 mL
¼ tsp.	freshly ground black pepper	1.2 mL

Combine the mayonnaise, sour cream, lemon juice and parsley in a food processor or blender. Process until smooth. Add the red peppers and process until semi-puréed. Season with salt and pepper. Transfer to a serving bowl, cover and chill.

The dip can be stored in an airtight container in the refrigerator for 5 days.

This tasty dip can be served with Sweet Potato Chips (see page 108), raw vegetables or tortilla chips.

You can roast your own peppers or purchase a jar of roasted red peppers to save time. Just drain the peppers and pat them dry before adding them to the dip. Light mayonnaise or sour cream can be used in this recipe.

Creamy Blue Cheese Dip

Makes 1 3/4 cups (420 mL)

A creamy, tangy dip
that uses Danish blue
cheese. For a change
of flavor, try an
imported English
Stilton or Italian
Gorgonzola. For a
lighter version, use a
low-fat mayonnaise,
low-fat sour cream or
plain yogurt.

1/2 cup	sour cream	120 mL
1/2 cup	mayonnaise	120 mL
5 oz.	Danish blue cheese, finely crumbled	140 g
1/8 tsp.	cayenne pepper	.5 mL
2 Tbsp.	finely chopped green onions	30 mL

In a food processor or blender, combine the sour cream, mayonnaise, blue cheese and cayenne pepper. Process until smooth. Transfer to a serving dish. Sprinkle with the green onions. Cover and refrigerate until serving time. The dip can be stored in an airtight container in the refrigerator for up to 5 days.

Spinach Dip

Makes 2 1/2 cups (600 mL)

1/2 cup	mayonnaise	120 mL
1/2 cup	sour cream	120 mL
1	3-oz. (85-g) package dry vegetable soup mixture	1
1/4 cup	chopped fresh parsley	60 mL
3	green onions, chopped	3
1	8-oz. (227-mL) can sliced water chestnuts, drained	1
1	10-oz. (284-mL) package frozen spinach, thawed	1
	salt and freshly ground black pepper to taste	
1	6-inch (15-cm) round loaf of bread	1

This dip is served in a hollowed-out loaf of crusty bread. For a pretty presentation, line a basket with a cloth napkin and place the hollowed bread inside, arranging the cubed bread around it. Tuck several sprigs of parsley and edible fresh flowers in the basket. To reduce the amount of fat in this recipe, substitute light mayonnaise or fat-free sour cream.

Combine the mayonnaise and sour cream in a large bowl. Stir in the vegetable soup mixture, parsley, green onions and water chestnuts. Squeeze out the excess water from the spinach and chop finely. Add to the mayonnaise mixture and stir well. Season with salt and pepper. Cover and refrigerate until ready to serve.

The dip can be stored in an airtight container in the refrigerator for 3 days.

With a serrated knife, cut a 1/2-inch (1.2-cm) slice from the top of the bread. Remove the bread from the inside of the shell, leaving about 1 inch (2.5 cm) of thickness all around. Cut the reserved bread into large cubes. Spoon the spinach mixture into the hollowed-out bread. Serve with the cubed bread for dipping.

Roasted Garlic Spread

Makes 6—8 servings

Garlic becomes very sweet and mellow as it roasts. Spread it on grilled country bread or crackers for a taste of the Mediterranean. Leftover garlic is a wonderful addition to dressings, soup, pasta sauces or any dish calling for garlic.

4	whole heads garlic	4
2 Tbsp.	olive oil	30 mL
1/2 tsp.	fresh thyme, or 1/4 tsp. (1.2 mL) dried	2.5 mL
	salt and freshly ground black pepper to taste	

Preheat the oven to 350ºF (175ºC).

Remove the papery outside layer of the garlic. Trim 1/4 inch (.6 cm) off the tops of the garlic heads. Place them in an ovenproof dish and brush with the oil. Sprinkle with thyme, salt and pepper. Cover the dish with foil and bake 1 1/2 hours, or until very tender.

Serve warm or at room temperature. To remove the garlic, gently squeeze it from the husks.

Baba Ghanoush

Makes 1½ cups (360 mL)

1	large eggplant, about 1½ lbs. (680 g)	1
2 Tbsp.	fresh lemon juice	30 mL
2 Tbsp.	tahini	30 mL
3	cloves garlic, minced	3
1 tsp.	salt	5 mL
2 Tbsp.	yogurt	30 mL
2 Tbsp.	olive oil	30 mL
2 Tbsp.	chopped pistachios (optional)	30 mL

This garlicky, lemony, roasted eggplant dip from the Middle East is served with wedges of pita bread and sprinkled with toasted pistachio nuts. Tahini—ground sesame seed paste—is available in the ethnic section of your supermarket. It will keep well in a glass jar in the refrigerator for up to 6 months after opening.

Preheat the oven to 400°F (200°C).

Cut the eggplant in half lengthwise, and prick the skin in several places with a fork. Place, cut side down, on a greased baking sheet. Bake 20–30 minutes, until it's tender and the skin is shriveled.

Set the eggplant aside to cool. Leave the skin on if you prefer a charred taste. Otherwise, remove the seeds and scoop out the pulp. Transfer the pulp to a food processor and add the lemon juice, tahini, garlic, salt, yogurt and oil. Process until smooth. Taste and add more lemon juice or salt to taste.

Transfer to a serving bowl and sprinkle with the chopped pistachios if desired. Serve warm or at room temperature. The dip can be stored in a covered container in the refrigerator for 3 days and brought back to room temperature before serving.

Green Goddess Dip

Makes 1½ cups (360 mL)

This dip is a variation on the classic green goddess dip found in many cookbooks. Buttermilk has replaced the anchovy fillets and the mixture is puréed to a smooth sauce. Serve with assorted raw vegetables or thin it with some milk and serve as a delicious dressing over sliced tomatoes. You can use a light or fat-free sour cream in this recipe without sacrificing flavor.

½ cup	sour cream	120 mL
¼ cup	buttermilk	60 mL
2 Tbsp.	white wine vinegar	30 mL
1 Tbsp.	lemon juice	15 mL
1 Tbsp.	chopped fresh tarragon, or 1 tsp. (5 ml) dried	15 mL
2 Tbsp.	chopped fresh parsley	30 mL
2 Tbsp.	chopped fresh dill, or 2 tsp. (10 mL) dried	30 mL
3 Tbsp.	finely chopped green onion	45 mL
1 Tbsp.	sugar	15 mL
¼ tsp.	salt	1.2 mL
⅛ tsp.	freshly ground black pepper	.5 mL
1 Tbsp.	chopped fresh chives	15 mL

In a large bowl, combine the sour cream, buttermilk, vinegar, lemon juice, tarragon, parsley, dill, green onion and sugar. Season with salt and pepper and mix well. Transfer to a serving bowl and sprinkle with the chives. Cover and chill until ready to serve.

The dip can be stored in an airtight container in the refrigerator for 5 days.

Cheddar Cheese Ball

Makes 6 servings

1	8-oz. (227-ml) package cream cheese, softened	1
2 cups	grated sharp Cheddar cheese	475 mL
1 tsp.	Worcestershire sauce	5 mL
1 tsp.	fresh lemon juice	5 mL
2 Tbsp.	chopped green onions	30 mL
1/4 tsp.	salt	1.2 mL
1/2 cup	walnuts, finely chopped	120 mL

This sharp, zesty cheese is rolled in chopped walnuts for a lovely presentation, but you can substitute pecans or finely chopped parsley if you like. Serve with assorted crackers, slices of tart apple, crunchy celery sticks and crisp cucumber rounds.

Beat the cream cheese until creamy in a food processor or electric mixer. Add the Cheddar cheese, Worcestershire sauce, lemon juice, green onions and salt. Cover and chill for 2 hours.

Remove the cheese mixture from the refrigerator. Shape it into a large ball and roll it in chopped walnuts. Place it on a serving platter, gently pressing it down on the platter to prevent it from sliding off. Serve at room temperature.

The cheese ball can be wrapped and stored for up to 3 days in the refrigerator. Bring it back to room temperature before serving.

Stilton Walnut Spread

Makes 1 1/2 cups (360 mL)

Stilton is a magnificent English blue-veined cheese, with a full rich flavor. Serve this chunky spread with crackers, crisp pear wedges and a glass of tawny port. Store unused cheese in the refrigerator, wrapped in plastic, for up to a month.

1/4 cup	mayonnaise	60 mL
1/4 cup	sour cream	60 mL
1/2 cup	crumbled Stilton cheese	120 mL
1/4 cup	coarsely chopped walnuts	60 mL
	walnut halves (optional)	

Process the mayonnaise and sour cream in a food processor or blender until smooth. Add the Stilton and walnuts and blend slightly (do not purée into a paste). Transfer to a serving dish. Garnish with the walnut halves if desired. Cover and chill 1 hour in the refrigerator prior to serving.

The dip can be stored in an airtight container in the refrigerator for 5 days and brought back to room temperature before serving.

Pesto Cheesecake

Makes 10 servings

A layered cheesecake is an impressive centerpiece for a buffet table. Serve it with sliced French bread and crackers, and garnish it with edible flowers and fresh herb sprigs.

1 1/2	8-oz. (225-g) packages cream cheese, softened	1 1/2
3 cups	grated Swiss cheese	720 mL
1/4 cup	sour cream	60 mL
1/2 cup	Pesto (page 168)	120 mL
1/4 cup	pine nuts, toasted	60 mL
2 Tbsp.	chopped fresh basil	30 mL

Line the bottom of an 8-inch (20-cm) springform pan with waxed paper.

Combine the cream cheese, Swiss cheese and sour cream in a food processor; process until smooth. Spread half the mixture in the bottom of the pan. Top with the pesto and cover with the remaining cheese mixture. Smooth evenly. Cover with plastic wrap and refrigerate for 3 hours or overnight.

To serve, remove the sides from the pan. Invert on a serving platter. Remove the bottom of the pan and the waxed paper. Sprinkle with the pine nuts and chopped basil. Serve at room temperature.

The cheesecake can be covered and stored in the refrigerator for 4 days. Bring it back to room temperature before serving.

Tuna Caper Pâté

Makes 3/4 cup (180 mL)

This is an easy, quick appetizer that can be served with rustic peasant bread, celery sticks or crisp radishes. Make sure to purchase canned tuna packed in olive oil (tonno sotto'olio) imported from Italy, which is available in most supermarkets. The tuna comes from the belly of the fish (the most tender and flavorful part).

1	6-oz. (170-g) can tuna, packed in olive oil	1
1 tsp.	capers, drained and rinsed	5 mL
2 Tbsp.	unsalted butter, cubed and softened	30 mL
1/4 tsp.	salt	1.2 mL
1/8 tsp.	freshly ground black pepper	.5 mL
1 tsp.	crushed multicolored peppercorns (optional)	5 mL

Combine the tuna and capers in a food processor or blender. Process into a coarse paste. With the motor running, add the butter gradually until you have a smooth paste. Scrape down the sides of the bowl. Season with salt and pepper. Transfer to a small crock and sprinkle with the crushed peppercorns, if desired. Serve chilled or at room temperature.

The pâté can be stored in an airtight container in the refrigerator for 5 days.

Capers

Capers are the salted or pickled flower bud of the caper bush, which grows wild in the Mediterranean. Rinse them under cold water to remove some of the salt. Use them in dips, sauces and salads.

Potted Salmon

Makes 1 1/2 cups (360 mL)

2 Tbsp.	butter or margarine	30 mL
1	small onion, chopped	1
10 oz.	fresh salmon fillet, cut into 1-inch (2.5-cm) cubes	285 g
2 Tbsp.	dry white wine	30 mL
1 Tbsp.	lemon juice	15 mL
1 tsp.	fresh thyme, or 1/8 tsp. (.5 mL) dried	5 mL
1	4-oz. (113-g) package cream cheese, softened	1
1/4 tsp.	salt	1.2 mL
1/8 tsp.	freshly ground black pepper	.5 mL

Melt the butter in a large non-stick frying pan over medium heat. Add the onion and cook about 5 minutes, until soft. Add the salmon cubes and white wine and cook for 3 minutes, or until the fish flakes with a fork. Cool slightly.

Combine the salmon, lemon juice and thyme in a food processor or blender. Add the cream cheese and blend until smooth. Season with salt and pepper. Transfer to a serving bowl. Cover and refrigerate until serving time.

The spread can be made 2 days in advance, stored in a covered container in the refrigerator and brought back to room temperature before serving.

Potted fish is a traditional old English spread that uses boneless haddock, cod or whitefish. I have used fresh salmon in this recipe, but you can also make it with canned sockeye salmon. If you use a canned salmon, remember to omit the salt, remove the bones and drain the salmon well. Serve this spread with melba toast, Scandinavian flat bread or poppyseed crackers.

Smoked Trout Mousse

Makes 1 cup (240 mL)

Serve this smoky, creamy spread with raw vegetables, piped on cucumber rounds or with sesame crackers.

8 oz.	smoked trout or whitefish	225 g
1 Tbsp.	fresh lemon juice	15 mL
1 Tbsp.	prepared horseradish	15 ml
1	8-oz. (225-g) package cream cheese	1
3 Tbsp.	whipping cream	45 mL
	salt and freshly ground black pepper to taste	
1 tsp.	chopped fresh dill (optional)	5 mL

Remove the skin and bones from the trout. Chop finely in a food processor. Add the lemon juice, horseradish, cream cheese and whipping cream. Process until smooth and creamy. Season with salt and pepper. Transfer to a serving bowl and sprinkle with the fresh dill if desired. Cover and chill until ready to serve.

The dip can be stored in an airtight container in the refrigerator for 3 days.

Hot Crab Dip

Makes 1 1/2 cups (360 mL)

1/4 cup	mayonnaise	60 mL
1	8-oz. (225-g) package cream cheese, softened	1
1/2 tsp.	cayenne pepper	2.5 mL
1/4 tsp.	salt	1.2 mL
1/8 tsp.	pepper	.5 ml
2	6-oz. (170-mL) cans crabmeat, drained and cartilage removed	2
1/4 cup	finely chopped green onions	60 mL
2 Tbsp.	chopped fresh parsley	30 mL

Sweet crabmeat is perfect in this creamy, delicious dip. Serve it with Pita Chips (page 166), Sesame Wonton Crackers (page 163) and raw vegetables.

Preheat the oven to 350ºF (175ºC).

Beat the mayonnaise, cream cheese, cayenne, salt and pepper until creamy in a food processor or electric mixer. Fold in the crab and green onions. Mix well. Transfer to a medium baking dish.

Bake for 20 minutes, or until bubbly and heated through. The dip can be made a day in advance, stored in a container in the refrigerator and warmed before serving. Sprinkle with the parsley just before serving.

Crabs

Dungeness crab is available fresh from October to May. You can find it canned or frozen year round. Spider crab, sometimes identified as snow crab, is sold canned and the legs are frozen. Carefully pick over crabmeat and remove any shells or cartilage. Frozen Alaskan king crab has more flavor and better texture than canned crabmeat. It is available frozen in your local supermarket. Thaw it in the refrigerator for several hours, and squeeze and blot it dry before using it in a recipe.

Cocktail Sauce

This sauce is a snap to make and can be used as a dipping sauce with cold poached shrimp. Sweet chili sauce is available at your local supermarket.

Makes 1/2 cup (120 mL)

1/2 cup	sweet chili sauce	120 mL
2 Tbsp.	ketchup	30 mL
1 tsp.	prepared horseradish	5 mL
1/2 tsp.	Worcestershire sauce	2.5 mL
1 tsp.	fresh lemon juice	5 mL

Combine all the ingredients and mix well. Cover and chill for 30 minutes before serving.

The sauce can be stored in an airtight container in the refrigerator for 2 weeks.

Facing page (from top): *Chinese Wontons (p. 44), Curried Chicken in Bouchées (p. 41), and Steamed Dumplings (p. 46).*

Shrimp Cocktail Spread

Makes 4–6 servings

3/4 cup	Cocktail Sauce (page 34)	180 mL
2 Tbsp.	finely chopped green onion	30 mL
1	8-oz. (225-g) package cream cheese, softened	1
8 oz.	cooked baby bay shrimp	225 g
2 tsp.	fresh lemon juice	10 mL
1 Tbsp.	chopped fresh dill	15 mL

Combine the cocktail sauce and green onion. Spread the cream cheese in a thick layer on a serving platter. Pour the sauce over the cheese, and top with the shrimp. Drizzle with lemon juice and sprinkle with the dill. Serve with a knife and a basket of assorted crackers.

This spread allows you to serve shrimp at a party without breaking your budget. If you don't want to make the cocktail sauce from scratch, purchase a high-quality brand you like. Cooked baby bay shrimp are available fresh or canned at local supermarkets.

Facing page (from top): *California Sushi Rolls (p. 59) and Smoked Salmon Sushi Rolls (p. 58).*

Swiss Fondue

Makes 8–10 servings

The secret to making a smooth fondue is to keep the heat just low enough that the cheese melts slowly. Overheating will make the cheese stringy. Kirsch is a brandy distilled from cherries and is produced in Alsace, Germany. If kirsch is unavailable, substitute a dry sherry.

4 cups	shredded Swiss or Gruyère cheese	950 mL
1 1/2 Tbsp.	cornstarch	22.5 mL
1 cup	dry white wine	240 mL
2 Tbsp.	Kirsch or dry sherry	30 mL
1/8 tsp.	ground nutmeg	.5 mL
1/8 tsp.	paprika	.5 mL
	freshly ground black pepper to taste	
2	loaves French bread, cut into 1/2-inch (1.2-cm) cubes	2

Combine the cheese and cornstarch in a large bowl. Heat the wine in a medium saucepan over medium-low heat. Add the cheese mixture in small amounts, stirring with a wooden spoon after each addition. When the cheese is completely melted and begins to bubble, add the kirsch or sherry, nutmeg, paprika and pepper.

Transfer the cheese to a fondue pot. Serve with the cubed bread.

If the fondue becomes too thick, thin it out with warm wine. If the fondue separates, mix 1 Tbsp. (15 mL) cornstarch with 1/4 cup (60 mL) wine, warm the mixture and add it to the fondue pot.

Beer and Cheddar Fondue

Makes 6 servings

2 cups	shredded Cheddar or Muenster cheese	475 mL
2 Tbsp.	all-purpose flour	30 ml
1	clove garlic, crushed	1
1	8-oz. (227-ml) bottle beer	1
1/2 tsp.	prepared mustard	2.5 mL
1 cup	each broccoli, cauliflower, green pepper, mushrooms	240 mL
1	loaf French bread cut into 1/2-inch (1.2-cm) cubes	1

Combine the cheese and flour. Toss well and set aside.

Rub the inside of a medium saucepan with the garlic clove; discard the garlic. Add the beer to the saucepan. Heat over medium heat until warm. Add the cheese mixture in small amounts, stirring each addition until melted. Stir in the mustard.

Pour the cheese into a fondue pot and keep it warm over a burner. Serve with assorted vegetables and cubes of bread.

If the fondue becomes too thick, thin it out with warm beer. If the fondue separates, mix 1 Tbsp. (15 mL) cornstarch with 1/4 cup (60 mL) beer, warm the mixture and add it to the fondue pot.

Making a fondue is an easy and fun way to entertain—and the vegetables can be prepared a day in advance. So dust off your fondue set and invite the gang over for a casual dining experience.

Wrapped, Rolled and Stuffed Finger Foods

This chapter showcases the hottest trend to hit North America—finger foods that are wrapped, rolled and stuffed. You can use a variety of wrappers available at your local grocery store: Japanese nori, Middle Eastern pita bread and phyllo, lettuce leaves, wonton wrappers, spring wrappers, rice paper wrappers and Mexican tortillas.

The recipes include classic ethnic favorites such as Japanese spring rolls, Mexican quesadillas, Greek spinach triangles and Chinese wontons. There are also modern adaptations—California sushi rolls, fennel-scented Italian crescents and curried tortilla rolls—which look spectacular and are easy to assemble.

Your guests will love to munch on these compact finger foods that can be made in advance or assembled just before your function.

Curried Chicken in Bouchées

Makes 36 pieces

This curried chicken mixture in tiny puff pastries makes an elegant and easy appetizer.

1 Tbsp.	vegetable oil	15 mL
1	small onion, sliced	1
1	clove garlic, minced	1
1 lb.	skinless, boneless chicken breasts, thinly sliced	455 g
1	14-oz. (398-mL) can diced plum tomatoes, drained	1
1 Tbsp.	honey	15 mL
2 Tbsp.	mild curry paste	30 mL
1/2 tsp.	salt	2.5 mL
1/8 tsp.	freshly ground black pepper	.5 mL
1 recipe	Bouchées (page 159)	1 recipe
36	cilantro sprigs	36

Heat the oil to medium-high in a large, non-stick frying pan. Add the onion and garlic and cook until tender. Add the chicken and cook until lightly browned. Mix in the tomatoes, honey and curry paste. Bring to a boil and cook for 5 minutes. Season with salt and pepper. Remove from the heat and let cool.

Spoon 1 Tbsp. (15 mL) of filling into each bouchée. Garnish with a cilantro sprig.

Curry Paste

Curry paste contains oil and is more fragrant than ground curry powder. It's available in the ethnic section of your local supermarket. Store unused paste in the refrigerator for up to 3 months.

Pork Pot Stickers with Sweet Soy Sauce

Makes approximately 60 pieces

Pot stickers are a popular snack food in northern China and get their name from the cooking method—pan-frying then steaming. These halfmoon-shaped dumplings stick to the pan and become golden on the bottom when fried. Don't worry if you tear a few when you remove them from the pan. The technique takes some practice.

1 lb.	lean ground pork	455 g
1/4 cup	oyster sauce	60 mL
1 Tbsp.	soy sauce	15 mL
2	cloves garlic, minced	2
1/4 cup	finely sliced green onions	60 mL
1/2 tsp.	cumin	2.5 mL
1 tsp.	chili sauce	5 mL
1/2 tsp.	freshly ground black pepper	2.5 mL
60	dumpling wrappers (see page 47)	60
1/4 cup	vegetable oil	60 mL
1 1/2 cups	cold water	360 mL
1/4 cup	sliced green onions	60 mL
1 recipe	Sweet Soy Sauce	1 recipe

Combine the pork, oyster sauce, soy sauce, garlic, 1/4 cup (60 mL) green onions, cumin, chili sauce and pepper.

Working in batches, arrange the wrappers on your work surface. Lightly brush the edges of each wrapper with warm water. Place a spoonful of filling in the center of each wrapper and fold it in half. Press the edges firmly to seal. Place the finished dumplings on a baking sheet and cover with waxed paper. Repeat with the remaining wrappers. The dumplings can be stored covered in the refrigerator up to 1 day or frozen in an airtight container for 1 month.

Heat 1 tsp. (5 mL) of the oil in a large non-stick frying pan over high heat. Arrange 10 dumplings in a single layer in the pan. Cook until the bottoms are nicely browned, shaking the pan to prevent sticking. Flip the dumplings over, add 1/4 cup (60 mL) of the water to the pan, cover and cook

3 minutes. Uncover and continue to cook until the water has evaporated, about 3 minutes.

Transfer the cooked dumplings to a large ovenproof dish. Place in a preheated 200°F (95°C) oven to keep warm. Cook the remaining dumplings, adding them to the pan in the oven as they are finished. Transfer the dumplings to a serving platter lined with lettuce leaves. Sprinkle with the remaining green onions and serve with Sweet Soy Sauce.

Sweet Soy Sauce
Makes ³/₄ cup (180 mL)

Serve this simple sweet sauce with pot stickers or as a dipping sauce for vegetable tempura. Mirin is a sweet Japanese rice wine, used in sauces or salad dressings. If mirin is unavailable, you can substitute dry sherry and 1 tsp. (5 mL) of sugar.

¹/₄ cup	soy sauce	60 mL
¹/₂ cup	mirin	120 mL
1 tsp.	sugar	5 mL
2 Tbsp.	water	30 mL

Combine all the ingredients. Cover and refrigerate for up to 5 days.

Chinese Wontons with Plum Dipping Sauce

Makes 30 wontons

These crispy Chinese wontons can be filled with delicate chopped vegetables, seasoned ground pork, chicken or beef. You can also serve them steamed or poached in chicken stock for a quick soup. Wonton wrappers are available in the specialty section of your supermarket or Asian food stores.

1/2 lb.	lean ground pork	225 g
1/4 cup	chopped green onions	60 mL
1 tsp.	red pepper flakes	5 mL
2	cloves garlic, minced	2
1	medium carrot, grated	1
2 Tbsp.	soy sauce	30 mL
1 tsp.	minced fresh ginger	5 mL
1/2	1-lb. (455-g) package square wonton wrappers	1/2
1	egg, beaten	1
1 recipe	Plum Dipping Sauce	1 recipe

Combine the pork, green onion, red pepper flakes, garlic, carrot, soy sauce and ginger and mix well. Arrange the wrappers on your work surface. Place 1 tsp. (5 mL) of filling in the center of each wrapper. With a small pastry brush, moisten the exposed edges with the egg wash. Bring the wrapper up over the filling, forming a triangle. Press gently to seal. Next, bring the two side points up over the filling, and overlap the points. Seal with beaten egg. Stand the wontons up on a baking sheet. The wontons can be stored wrapped for 1 day or frozen for 1 month.

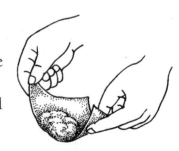

To cook, heat 1 inch (2.5 cm) of vegetable oil in a wok or deep pot to 375°F (190°C). Fry the wontons for about 1 minute on each side. Drain on paper towels. Wontons can be fried ahead of time and reheated in a 400°F (200°C) oven for 10 minutes. Serve hot with the plum sauce.

Plum Dipping Sauce

Makes ³/₄ cup (180 mL)

As well as a wonderful dipping sauce with crispy wontons, this is a great baste to brush on grilled chicken and pork saté.

¹/₄ cup	hoisin sauce	60 mL
¹/₂ cup	plum sauce	120 mL
1 tsp.	soy sauce	5 mL
1 Tbsp.	rice vinegar	15 mL
1 Tbsp.	honey	15 mL
1 tsp.	Dijon mustard	5 mL
1 Tbsp.	water	15 mL

Mix all the ingredients together, cover and refrigerate until ready to serve. The dip can be stored in an airtight container in the refrigerator for 5 days.

Steamed Dumplings

Makes 36 dumplings

These fragrant steamed dumplings are simple to make. If you don't have a bamboo steamer, line a metal colander with lettuce leaves, cover it with a lid and place directly over a pot of simmering water. Serve with Spicy Dipping Sauce.

1 Tbsp.	vegetable oil	15 mL
1	small onion, finely chopped	1
2	cloves garlic, minced	2
1 Tbsp.	chopped ginger	15 mL
1 cup	finely chopped mushrooms	240 mL
1/4 cup	grated carrot	60 mL
2 Tbsp.	soy sauce	30 mL
1 tsp.	sesame oil	5 mL
2 Tbsp.	chopped fresh cilantro	30 mL
1/8 tsp.	pepper	.5 mL
36	dumpling wrappers	36
	lettuce leaves	
	chive blossoms (optional)	
1/4 cup	Spicy Dipping Sauce (page 64)	60 mL

Heat the oil to medium-high in a large, non-stick frying pan. Add the onion, garlic and ginger and cook about 5 minutes, or until soft and fragrant. Add the mushrooms and cook until tender. Transfer to a large bowl and add the carrot, soy sauce, sesame oil, cilantro and pepper. Toss gently.

Lay out as many dumpling wrappers as you have room for on your work surface. Lightly brush the edges of each wrapper with warm water. Place a heaping spoonful of filling in the center of each. Fold the wrapper in half and press the edges firmly to seal. Place the finished dumplings on a baking sheet and cover with waxed paper.

Repeat with the remaining wrappers. The dumplings can be frozen on the baking sheet, transferred to an airtight container and kept in the freezer for 2 months.

To cook the dumplings, line a bamboo steamer with lettuce (this prevents the dumplings from sticking). Arrange the dumplings in a single layer over the lettuce and cover with the lid. Place over a pot of simmering water and steam for 12 minutes. Repeat with the remaining dumplings. Arrange on a platter with chive blossoms. Serve immediately with the dipping sauce.

Dumpling Wrappers

Dumpling wrappers are called *sue-gow* in Chinese. They are round, thin wrappers, sold fresh or frozen in Asian food stores and some supermarkets. Once open, the wrappers can be rewrapped in plastic and stored in the refrigerator for 1 week. Substitute wonton wrappers if dumpling wrappers are unavailable.

Beef and Tomato Empanadas

Empanadas, spicy little turnovers stuffed with a ground meat mixture, are a favorite snack food in Chile. Serve them with sour cream or a fresh tomato salsa.

Makes 40 empanadas

1 Tbsp.	olive oil	15 mL
1/2 lb.	lean ground beef	225 g
1	small onion, finely chopped	1
2	cloves garlic, minced	2
1	28-oz. (796-mL) can diced plum tomatoes, drained	1
1/2 cup	sultana raisins, soaked and drained	120 mL
1 Tbsp.	cumin	15 mL
1	jalapeño pepper, finely chopped	1
	salt and freshly ground black pepper to taste	
1/2 recipe	Basic Pastry Dough (see page 157)	1/2 recipe
1	egg, slightly beaten	1

Heat the oil in a large non-stick frying pan over medium-high heat. Add the beef, breaking it up with a wooden spoon until cooked, about 3 minutes. Add the onion and garlic and cook until tender. Drain off any fat if necessary.

Add the tomatoes, raisins, cumin and jalapeño. Bring to a boil. Reduce the heat and cook gently for about 10 minutes. Season with salt and pepper.

The mixture should not be runny; pour off extra juice if necessary. Transfer the mixture to a bowl and let cool. It can be made one day in advance and stored, covered, in the refrigerator.

Preheat the oven to 350ºF (175ºC).

On a lightly floured board, roll out the dough to 1/8-inch (.3-cm) thickness. Cut the dough into 2 1/2-inch (6-cm) rounds, using a cookie cutter. Place a spoonful of the beef filling in the center of each pastry round. Moisten the edges with cold water. Fold the pastry in half. Seal the edges with the tines of a fork. Prick the top of each turnover several times with a fork.

Place the turnovers on a lightly greased baking sheet. Brush the tops with the beaten egg. Bake for 15–20 minutes, or until golden. Serve warm or at room temperature.

The empanadas can be made ahead of time and stored in an airtight container in the freezer for 3 months. Warm them in the oven before serving.

Crispy Italian Sausage Crescents

Makes approximately 36

These light, flaky sausage crescents melt in your mouth and leave a hint of fennel. Fennel seeds have a sweet, licorice flavor that is very similar to anise, but much milder. It is used in Italian sausage or added to Indian curry dishes. The crescents can be served with a dipping sauce—try Fresh Tomato Sauce (page 169) or Pesto Dip (page 19).

2 Tbsp.	olive oil	30 mL
1	large onion, finely chopped	1
1/2 tsp.	fennel seeds, toasted	2.5 mL
1/2 lb.	spicy Italian sausage, casing removed and meat crumbled	225 g
1/4 tsp.	salt	1.2 mL
1/4 tsp.	pepper	1.2 mL
1	1-lb. (455-g) package puff pastry, thawed	1
1	egg, lightly beaten	1

Heat the oil in a large, non-stick frying pan. Add the onion and cook for 7 minutes, or until soft and fragrant. Add the fennel and sausage. Cook until the meat is no longer pink. Drain off the fat. Season with salt and pepper. Set aside.

On a lightly floured board, roll out the puff pastry to 1/8-inch (.3-cm) thickness. Cut the dough with a round 2 1/2-inch (6-cm) cookie cutter. Place a spoonful of beef filling in the center of each pastry round. Brush the edges with beaten egg. Fold the pastry over the filling and press to seal. Brush the tops of the pastry with the remaining beaten egg. The crescents can be made to this point ahead of time and stored unbaked in the refrigerator for up to 12 hours or frozen for 1 month.

Preheat the oven to 400°F (200°C). Place the crescents on a parchment-lined baking sheet. Bake for 15 minutes, or until puffed and golden brown. Serve immediately.

Facing page: *Red Pepper and Pesto Tortilla Rolls (p. 67).*

Following page: *Chicken and Green Pepper Kebabs (p. 76).*

Calzone

Makes 4 servings

2 Tbsp.	olive oil	30 mL
1/4 cup	sliced onion	60 mL
3	Roma tomatoes, chopped	3
1	red pepper, sliced into strips	1
1	green pepper, sliced into strips	1
1/2 cup	ricotta cheese	120 mL
1 Tbsp.	chopped fresh basil	15 mL
1/2 cup	grated mozzarella cheese	120 mL
	salt and freshly ground black pepper to taste	
1	1-lb. (455-g) package frozen bread dough, thawed	1

These half-moon pizza turnovers are easy to assemble. Ricotta cheese, an Italian-style cottage cheese, is available in the dairy case of your local supermarket.

Heat the oil to medium-high in a large frying pan. Add the onion and cook 4 minutes, or until soft. Add the tomatoes and red and green pepper and cook for 2 minutes. Remove from the heat and let cool.

Combine the ricotta cheese, basil and mozzarella cheese. Add the onion mixture and mix well. Season with salt and pepper.

Preheat the oven to 350°F (175°C).

With a knife, divide the dough into 4 pieces. On a lightly floured surface, roll each piece into a circle approximately 6 inches (15 cm) in diameter. Place the filling on one side of the circle. Fold the other half over top and pinch the edges shut. Make a hole on the top of each turnover to allow the steam to escape. Place the calzones on a greased baking sheet and brush with olive oil. Bake uncovered for 20 minutes. Serve warm.

Wild Mushroom Turnovers

These flaky-buttery turnovers are my childhood favorite. The recipe has been updated with the use of cultivated wild mushrooms, which are easily available at your local supermarket.

Makes about 60 pieces

1	8-oz. (225-g) package cream cheese, softened	1
1/2 cup	butter or margarine, softened	120 mL
2 cups	all-purpose flour	475 mL
2 Tbsp.	butter	30 mL
1	medium onion, finely chopped	1
1	clove garlic, minced	1
1 cup	crimini mushrooms, finely chopped	240 mL
1/2 cup	shiitake mushrooms, finely chopped	120 mL
1 cup	portobello mushrooms, finely chopped	240 mL
2 Tbsp.	brandy or dry sherry	30 mL
2 Tbsp.	all-purpose flour	30 mL
1 tsp.	salt	5 mL
1/4 tsp.	pepper	1.2 mL
1/4 cup	sour cream	60 mL
1	egg, beaten	1

In a large bowl, cream the cheese and 1/2 cup (120 mL) butter. Add the flour and gather the dough into a ball. Divide into 2 flat disks and wrap in plastic wrap. Cover and chill for 1 hour or up to 2 days.

Melt the 2 Tbsp. (30 mL) butter in a large frying pan over medium-high heat. Add the onion and garlic, and cook until soft and fragrant. Add the mushrooms and brandy or sherry. Cook until soft. Stir in the flour and cook for 2 minutes, or until the mixture thickens slightly. Season with salt and pepper. Remove from the heat and blend in the sour cream. Let cool. The mushroom filling can be made 1 day in advance and stored in an airtight container in the refrigerator.

Preheat the oven to 375°F (190°C).

On a lightly floured surface, roll the cream cheese dough to 1/8-inch (.3-cm) thickness. Cut into 3-inch (7.5-cm) circles. Brush the edges with the beaten egg. Place 1 tsp. (5 mL) of filling on each round. Fold in half and crimp the edges with the tines of a fork. Prick the tops with a fork in several places. Place on a baking sheet lined with parchment paper. Brush the tops with the remaining beaten egg. Bake for 15–20 minutes or until golden. Transfer to a platter and serve warm.

The turnovers can be made in advance and frozen baked or unbaked for up to 1 month. Reheat frozen baked turnovers in a preheated 350°F (175°C) oven for 7 minutes.

Choosing and Storing Mushrooms

Look for fresh mushrooms that are firm, plump and bruise-free. The underside of the gills should be closed, as open gills are a sign they are getting old. Store unwashed mushrooms in a brown paper bag in the refrigerator for up to 2 days. Do not store them in a plastic bag—they will become slimy and shrivel up due to lack of oxygen. To prepare mushrooms, gently wipe them clean with a damp cloth or soft brush. If they are extremely dirty, rinse them under cold water. If you soak them in water, they will become soft and slimy. Pat them dry with paper towels.

Portobello. Giant-sized mature crimini mushrooms. Remove the gills with a spoon before cooking to prevent the dish from turning black. They are excellent marinated and grilled.

Crimini. Brown button mushrooms with an earthy flavor that is stronger than the white variety.

Enoki. Oriental variety of mushrooms with a long slender stem and a tiny cap. They have a mild flavor and are excellent raw. Trim off the base to serve.

Shiitake. Japanese mushroom that grows on trees, and has a smoky, woody flavor. Cook the caps and save the stems for stock.

Oyster. Pale cream color, large cap, with a hint of oyster flavor. Best cooked with strong seasonings.

Spinach and Feta Triangles

Makes approximately 50 pieces

Phyllo is paper-thin dough that can be formed into different shapes and wrapped around delicious fillings. The recipe is for classic *tiropetes*, or triangles, filled with spinach and feta cheese. Phyllo is available in the frozen section of your local supermarket. A package contains 20 sheets and must be thawed in the refrigerator for several hours or overnight. When working with the pastry, use one sheet at a time and keep the rest covered with a damp tea towel to prevent drying.

1	10-oz. (285-g) package frozen chopped spinach	1
2 Tbsp.	olive oil	30 mL
1/4 cup	sliced green onion	60 mL
1 cup	feta cheese, crumbled	240 mL
1/4 cup	chopped fresh parsley	60 mL
1/4 cup	chopped fresh dill	60 mL
1	egg	1
	freshly ground black pepper to taste	
10	sheets phyllo	10
1/2 cup	melted butter	120 mL

Cook the spinach for 4 minutes. Drain and squeeze out excess water. Combine the spinach, olive oil, onion, feta cheese, parsley, dill and egg. Mix well. Season with pepper and set aside.

Place one sheet of phyllo on your work surface. Cover the remaining sheets with a damp tea towel. With a sharp knife cut the sheet lengthwise into 5 even strips. Using a pastry brush, brush the phyllo lightly with melted butter.

Place a heaping spoonful of filling onto the end of each strip. Form a triangle by folding 1 corner over the filling.

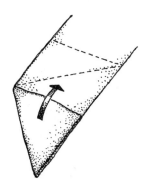

Continue folding upwards and sideways to the end of the strip.
Repeat with the remaining pastry.

Preheat the oven to 375°F (190°C). Arrange the triangles on
a lightly greased baking sheet. Brush the tops lightly with
butter. Bake for 20 minutes, or until golden brown. Serve hot.

The triangles can be frozen uncooked on a baking sheet,
transferred to an airtight container and kept in the freezer for
1 month. Bake the frozen triangles as above.

Sushi Rolls

Nori is seaweed that has been dried, pulverized, and then pressed into thin sheets. Look for pre-toasted sheets. If these are unavailable, you can quickly toast sheets over a burner for 3 seconds, or until they are crispy and have changed color slightly.

The idea of making sushi may seem a bit daunting at first. But with some practice and a few messy pieces they are quite easy to make. Practice making the rolls prior to your party and have some patience. I find the trick to producing these delectable seaweed-wrapped rolls is to make sure your rice is not too wet. And do not put too much sushi rice on the sheets of nori, or the rice will ooze out when you begin to roll them up. Sudari mats are bamboo mats used to roll up the sushi. They are available in Japanese markets and most supermarkets.

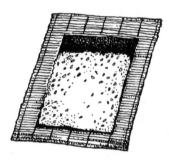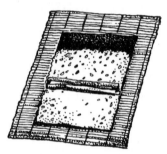

Distribute the rice over the nori sheet, leaving a ¹/₂-inch (1.2-cm) margin at the top. Lay the ingredients in strips across the rice.

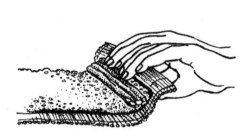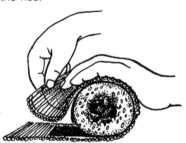

Hold the bottom edge of the mat with your thumbs and the ingredients with your fingers. Roll the bottom edge of the mat over the ingredients so that the bottom edge of the nori is touching the rice on the other side of the ingredients. Press the mat to tighten the roll and lift the mat out of the way, ending up with the seam on the bottom. Press the mat around the roll to shape it. With the roll seam side down, slice with a sharp knife.

Sushi Rice

Makes 4 cups (950 mL)

1/3 cup	plus 1 tsp. (5 mL) rice vinegar	80 mL
3 Tbsp.	sugar	45 mL
4 tsp.	salt	20 mL
3 1/4 cups	short-grain rice	780 mL
4 cups	water	950 mL

Combine the rice vinegar, sugar and salt in a small pot and bring to a boil. Remove from the heat and let cool.

Rinse the rice under cold running water until the water runs clear. Place the rice in a heavy saucepan and add the water. Cover and let soak for 15 minutes. Bring to a boil and let cool for 4 minutes. Reduce the heat to low and cook the rice for 15 minutes. Remove from the heat and let stand for 10 minutes. Do not remove the lid during the process.

Using a flat wooden spoon, spread the rice in a bowl. Slowly add the vinegar mixture while tossing the rice. Continue to toss the rice, cooling it with a fan while you are tossing it. This will take about 10 minutes.

The sushi rice can be covered with a damp tea towel and left at room temperature for up to 12 hours.

Short-grain Japanese white rice is seasoned with sweet rice vinegar to produce a sticky consistency that is the foundation of sushi making. I like to use Koko Rose rice from Japan, which is available in Asian markets and most supermarkets. Gently fanning the rice as it cools will produce a nice sheen. Enlist a friend to help in the process.

Smoked Salmon Sushi Roll

Kappa-maki is the
Japanese name for a
cucumber sushi roll. I
have added smoked
salmon in this elegant
version. For a quick
dipping sauce, mix
Japanese soy sauce
with a small amount
of wasabi.

Makes 32 pieces

4 sheets	pre-toasted nori	4
2 cups	cooked Sushi Rice (page 57)	475 mL
2 Tbsp.	powdered wasabi, mixed with 2 tsp. (10 mL) cold water	30 mL
4 oz.	smoked salmon, cut into strips	113 g
1	English cucumber, seeded and cut into strips	1

Place one nori sheet, shiny side down, on a bamboo sushi mat.
Distribute 1/2 cup (120 mL) of the rice over the nori sheet,
leaving a 1/2-inch (1.2-cm) margin at the top.

Dampen your hands with cold water and press the rice onto
the nori. (See illustration on page 56.) Spread a thin layer of
wasabi along the center of the rice. Cover the wasabi with 1/4 of
the smoked salmon and cucumber. Lift the edge of the mat
with your thumbs. Hold the ingredients in place with your
fingers and roll the mat and nori to enclose the filling. Roll to
the far edge of the rice, stopping at the uncovered portion of
nori. Moisten the edge of the nori with water, and complete the
roll. Wrap the mat completely around the rice roll; press gently
for a few seconds. Unroll the mat. Repeat with the remaining
sheets of nori.

Cut each roll into 3/4-inch (2-cm) slices, wiping the knife
between cuts. Arrange the rolls on a serving platter. Serve with
soy sauce. The sushi rolls can be made 8 hours in advance.
Wrap them in plastic wrap and refrigerate until serving time.

Wasabi

Wasabi is sometimes referred to as Japanese horseradish, and is the root of the
wasabi plant. It comes in a powdered form or as a paste. Mix the powder with
cold water or a little rice vinegar. The longer you mix the wasabi the stronger it
becomes. It is available in Asian grocery stores or some supermarkets.

California Sushi Roll

Makes 32 pieces

4 sheets	pretoasted nori	4
2 cups	cooked Sushi Rice (page 57)	475 mL
2 Tbsp.	powdered wasabi, mixed with 2 tsp. (10 mL) cold water	30 mL
2	avocados, peeled and sliced into 1/4-inch (.6-cm) slices	1
1	red bell pepper, sliced thinly	1
6 oz.	crabmeat	170 g

Delicate sheets of nori encase fragrant seasoned rice, velvety avocado, sweet red bell pepper and crabmeat for a taste sensation. Arrange the sushi on a platter and accompany it with a mound of pungent wasabi and sliced Japanese pickled ginger.

Place a nori sheet, shiny side down, on a bamboo sushi mat. Distribute 1/2 cup (120 mL) of the rice over the nori sheet, leaving a 1/2-inch (1.2-cm) margin at the top.

Dampen your hands with cold water and press the rice onto the nori. (See illustration on page 56.) Spread a thin layer of wasabi along the center of the rice. Cover the wasabi with 1/4 of the avocado, red pepper and crabmeat. Lift the edge of the mat with your thumbs. Hold the ingredients in place with your fingers and roll the mat and nori to enclose the filling. Roll to the far edge of the rice, stopping at the uncovered portion of nori. Moisten the edge of the nori with water, and complete the roll. Wrap the mat completely around the rice roll; press gently for a few seconds. Unroll the mat. Repeat with the remaining sheets of nori.

Cut each roll into 3/4-inch (2-cm) slices, wiping the knife between cuts. Arrange the rolls on a serving platter. The rolls can be made ahead of time. Wrap them in plastic wrap and refrigerate for up to 8 hours.

Japanese Spring Rolls

Makes 24 rolls

These crispy, Japanese-inspired spring rolls can be made well in advance and frozen. The ground pork or chicken filling is marinated in a tart, sweet sauce, then cooked and tossed with crisp vegetables. Serve the rolls with Plum Dipping Sauce (page 45) for a sweet flavor, or cool Spicy Dipping Sauce (page 64). For a change, substitute ground chicken for the ground pork.

2 Tbsp.	soy sauce	30 mL
2 Tbsp.	oyster sauce	30 mL
1 tsp.	sugar	5 mL
1 Tbsp.	rice vinegar	15 mL
1/2 lb.	ground pork	225 g
2 Tbsp.	vegetable oil	30 mL
1	small onion, finely chopped	1
1	clove garlic, minced	1
1 Tbsp.	chopped fresh ginger	15 mL
1 cup	bean sprouts	240 mL
2	stalks celery, finely diced	2
1 cup	mushrooms, finely sliced	240 mL
	salt and freshly ground black pepper to taste	
1	package frozen 6-inch (15-cm) spring roll wrappers, thawed	1
1	egg, slightly beaten	1

Place the soy sauce, oyster sauce, sugar and rice vinegar in a bowl and toss with the ground pork. Cover and marinate for 30 minutes in the refrigerator.

Heat 1 Tbsp. (15 mL) of the oil to medium-high in a wok or large frying pan. Add the onion, garlic and ginger and cook until tender and soft, about 5 minutes. Add the marinated pork and cook until it's browned. Drain off the fat. With a slotted spoon, transfer the mixture to a bowl.

Add the remaining 1 Tbsp. (15 mL) oil to the frying pan. Cook the bean sprouts and celery for 4 minutes, until tender-crisp. Add the mushrooms and cook for 3 minutes longer.

Remove from the heat. Season with salt and pepper. Do not overcook the vegetables or they will be soggy in the wrapper. Drain off the excess liquid to prevent tearing and cracking of the spring roll wrappers.

Combine the vegetables and the pork mixture. Cool in the refrigerator for 1 hour or up to 1 day. The filling must be cold prior to filling the wrappers.

Separate the spring roll wrappers and cover with a slightly damp cloth (see page 63 for wrapping illustration). Working with one wrapper at a time, place the wrapper with a corner towards you. Place a large spoonful of filling in the center of the wrapper. Fold the bottom corner up and over the filling. Brush the corners with the beaten egg. Roll up into a cylinder, tucking in the sides. Place on a baking sheet and cover with wax paper. Repeat with the remaining filling.

Heat 1 inch (2.5 cm) of oil in a wok or deep pot to 375°F (190°C). Cook 3 spring rolls at a time, frying them for 2 minutes on each side until golden brown. Remove with a slotted spoon and drain on paper towels. Serve with a dipping sauce.

Spring rolls can be fried ahead of time and frozen in an airtight container for 1 month. Reheat in a 400°F (200°C) oven for 15 minutes, or until hot.

Note: For a low-fat alternative to frying, brush the spring rolls with beaten egg white. Place on a baking sheet lined with parchment paper and bake in a preheated 375°F (190°C) oven for 10 minutes, or until crispy.

Vegetable Spring Rolls with Spicy Dipping Sauce

Makes 24 pieces

Spring roll wrappers can be purchased fresh or frozen in your supermarket. Thaw them in the refrigerator to prevent them from cracking and use them within 3 days. Look for a wrapper that does not appear dry around the outer edges and try to work quickly when rolling them up. Hoisin sauce is a sweet, thick sauce made from fermented soybeans. It is readily available at your local supermarket or Chinese food store.

2 Tbsp.	vegetable oil	30 mL
1	medium onion, finely chopped	1
2	cloves garlic, minced	2
1 Tbsp.	peeled, finely chopped fresh ginger	15 mL
1/2 cup	sliced shiitake mushrooms	120 mL
1/4 cup	chopped Savoy cabbage	60 mL
1	4-oz. (113-g) can water chestnuts, drained and chopped	1
1/4 cup	chopped unsalted peanuts	60 mL
1/4 cup	hoisin sauce	60 mL
2 Tbsp.	soy sauce	30 mL
24	spring roll wrappers	24
1	egg, well beaten	1
1 recipe	Spicy Dipping Sauce	1 recipe

Heat the oil to medium-high in a wok or large frying pan. Add the onion, garlic and ginger and cook for 5 minutes, or until tender. Add the mushrooms and cabbage and cook for 2 minutes. Mix in the water chestnuts, peanuts, hoisin sauce and soy sauce. Transfer the mixture to a bowl and cool slightly.

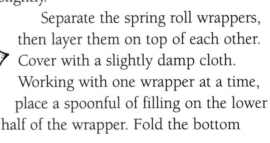

Separate the spring roll wrappers, then layer them on top of each other. Cover with a slightly damp cloth. Working with one wrapper at a time, place a spoonful of filling on the lower half of the wrapper. Fold the bottom

corner up and over the filling. Brush
the edges of each side with beaten
egg. Fold in the sides. Roll up and
press to seal. Place the rolls on a
baking sheet and cover with waxed
paper. Repeat with the remaining
filling. The rolls can be stored
covered in the refrigerator for 1 day
or frozen in an airtight container for
1 month.

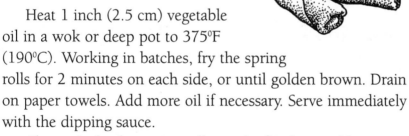

Heat 1 inch (2.5 cm) vegetable
oil in a wok or deep pot to 375°F
(190°C). Working in batches, fry the spring
rolls for 2 minutes on each side, or until golden brown. Drain
on paper towels. Add more oil if necessary. Serve immediately
with the dipping sauce.

Alternatively, the spring rolls can be fried several hours
ahead of time and reheated in a 400°F (200°C) oven for
10 minutes.

Spicy Dipping Sauce

Makes 1/2 cup (120 mL)

Increase the heat by adding additional sambal oelek or any other chili paste. Sambal oelek is ground, fresh red chilies with salt and vinegar added. Use it sparingly in dips, sauces and soups. Once open, sambal oelek will keep indefinitely in the refrigerator. It is available in supermarkets or Asian grocery stores.

1/4 cup	rice vinegar	60 mL
1 tsp.	sambal oelek	5 mL
1/4 cup	cold water	60 mL
1 Tbsp.	sugar	15 mL

Whisk all the ingredients together. Cover and refrigerate until ready to serve. The dip can be stored in an airtight container in the refrigerator for 3 days.

Soft Spring Rolls with Lime Dipping Sauce

Makes 4 servings

These fresh-tasting, low-fat rolls are called *poh piu* in Vietnamese cooking. Rice paper wrappers are rolled around assorted fillings and served uncooked with a dipping sauce. The wrappers are available in two sizes and shapes and can be found in the ethnic section of your local supermarket or Asian food stores.

2 oz.	dried rice noodles	57 g
8	8-inch (20-cm) round rice paper wrappers	8
8	small lettuce leaves, ribs removed	8
1	large carrot, grated	1
1/4 cup	chopped fresh cilantro	60 mL
2 Tbsp.	chopped fresh mint	30 mL
1/2	English cucumber, thinly sliced	1/2
24	shrimp, cooked, peeled and cut in half (page 118)	24
1 recipe	Lime Dipping Sauce (page 66)	1 recipe

Bring a small saucepan of water to a boil. Add the rice noodles
and cook for 3 minutes. Drain and rinse under cold water
to cool.

Dip one rice paper wrapper for
10 seconds in a bowl of warm water
(discard any wrappers that are
cracked). Place the wrapper on a work
surface covered with a damp tea towel.
Place a lettuce leaf in the center of the
wrapper. Top with cooked rice noodles,
carrot, cilantro, mint and cucumber. Fold up

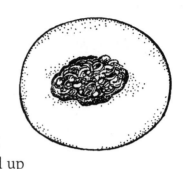

the bottom 1/3 of the wrapper to cover the
lettuce. Place 6 shrimp halves, cut side
down, over top of the wrapper. Roll
the wrapper up tightly, tucking in the
sides. Place seam side down on a
platter and cover with a damp tea
towel while you make the rest
of the spring rolls.

Serve with Lime Dipping Sauce. The rolls can be made
4 hours in advance and kept covered in the refrigerator.

Lime Dipping Sauce

Makes 3/4 cup (180 mL)

This tart sauce is also tasty with shrimp toasts or sprinkled over a bowl of steamed rice. Fresh chilies can be added if you prefer some heat.

2 Tbsp.	sugar	30 mL
1/2 cup	cold water	120 mL
1 Tbsp.	fish sauce (see page 136)	15 mL
1 Tbsp.	fresh lime juice	15 mL
1	cilantro leaf (optional)	1

Combine the sugar and water in a small saucepan and bring to a boil, stirring until the sugar dissolves. Remove from the heat. Stir in the fish sauce and lime juice. Pour into a small bowl. Garnish with a cilantro leaf if desired.

The sauce can be stored in an airtight container in the refrigerator for 5 days.

Facing page: *Chicken Tostaditas with Black Bean and Corn Salsa (p. 92).*

Following page (from top): *Parmesan Cheese Straws (p. 99) and Brie en Croute (p. 152).*

Red Pepper and Pesto Tortilla Rolls

Makes 32 pieces

1	8-oz. (225-g) package cream cheese, softened	1	
1/4 cup	Pesto (page 168)	60 mL	
4	8-inch (20-cm) flour tortillas	4	
1	large red bell pepper, roasted	1	
1 cup	fresh spinach leaves	240 mL	
1/2 cup	alfalfa sprouts	120 mL	

These soft tortilla rolls are quick and easy to prepare and look spectacular when arranged on a decorative platter. If you are pressed for time, use store-bought pesto and roasted red peppers.

Combine the cream cheese and pesto and mix well.

Arrange the tortillas on your work surface. Spread the cream cheese mixture evenly over each tortilla, leaving a 1/2-inch (1.2-cm) border around the edge. Place several red pepper strips along the center of the tortilla. Place the spinach and alfalfa sprouts over the red bell pepper. Roll up tightly. Cover in plastic wrap and refrigerate for 4 hours or up to 1 day.

Cut each tortilla crosswise into 8 1-inch (2.5-cm) slices. Arrange cut side up on a serving platter.

How to Roast Peppers

Grill peppers on an open flame until blistered and slightly charred, or roast or broil in a 450°F (230°C) oven. Turn the peppers to blacken them on all sides. Place in a paper bag to cool. When cool enough to handle, peel off the skin and discard the seeds. The peppers can be frozen in a freezer bag for up to 6 months.

Smoked Ham and Swiss Cheese Tortilla Rolls

Makes 32 pieces

Tortillas are very versatile and can be turned into a quick appetizer. Look for spinach or sun-dried tomato tortillas in your local supermarket. If unavailable, use plain flour tortillas.

1	8-oz. (225-g) package cream cheese, softened	1
1/4 cup	finely sliced green onions	60 mL
1 tsp.	Dijon mustard	5 mL
1 cup	grated Swiss cheese	240 mL
4 oz.	thinly sliced smoked ham or turkey	113 g
4	lettuce leaves	4
4	8-inch (20-cm) spinach or sun-dried tomato tortillas	4

Combine the cream cheese, green onions and Dijon mustard in a small bowl.

Arrange the tortillas on your work surface. Spread the cream cheese mixture evenly over each tortilla, leaving a 1/2-inch (1.2-cm) border around the edge. Sprinkle with the grated Swiss cheese. Place the ham or turkey over the cheese. Arrange the lettuce over the turkey. Roll up tightly. Cover in plastic wrap and refrigerate for 4 hours or up to 1 day.

Cut each tortilla crosswise into 8 1-inch (2.5-cm) slices. Arrange cut side up on a serving platter.

Tomato and Cheddar Quesadillas

Makes 16 pieces

4	8-inch (20-cm) flour tortillas	4
1¹/2 cups	grated cheddar cheese	360 mL
3/4 cup	homemade or store-bought salsa	180 mL
1/4 cup	finely chopped green onions	60 mL
1 Tbsp.	chopped fresh cilantro	15 mL
2 tsp.	vegetable oil	10 mL

A quesadilla is a Mexican sandwich made with a tortilla and filled with cheese (queso) and any other filling. Serve fresh tomato salsa and sour cream alongside the quesadilla.

Place the tortillas on your work surface. Sprinkle half of each tortilla with cheese, salsa, green onions and cilantro. Fold the tortilla in half and press gently to seal.

Heat 1 tsp. (5 mL) oil to medium-high in a large, non-stick frying pan. Add 2 quesadillas and cook for 2 minutes, or until lightly browned. Turn them over and cook for another 2 minutes. Repeat with the other 2 quesadillas. Cut each quesadilla into 4 wedges. Serve immediately.

Smoked Salmon Quesadillas with Mango Grapefruit Salsa

Makes 16 pieces

These grilled Mexican sandwiches make a delicious appetizer served with a bowl of fresh-tasting fruit salsa. Substitute smoked turkey or ham if smoked salmon is unavailable.

1	4-oz. (113-g) package cream cheese, softened	1
1 tsp.	fresh lemon juice	5 mL
2 Tbsp.	lemon zest, finely chopped	30 mL
1 Tbsp.	chopped fresh dill	15 mL
4	8-inch (20-cm) flour tortillas	4
4 oz.	smoked salmon, thinly sliced	113 g
1/4 cup	finely diced red onion	60 mL
2 tsp.	vegetable oil	10 mL
1 recipe	Mango Grapefruit Salsa	1 recipe

Combine the cream cheese, lemon juice, lemon zest and dill.

Arrange the tortillas on your work surface and spread the cream cheese mixture evenly over half of each tortilla. Place the smoked salmon on top of the cheese. Sprinkle with red onion. Fold each tortilla in half and gently press to seal.

Heat 1 tsp. (5 mL) of the oil to medium-high in a large, non-stick frying pan. Place 2 tortillas in the pan and cook for 1 minute, until they're lightly browned. Turn them over and cook for 1 minute, until they're brown and the filling is warm. Repeat with the remaining oil and tortillas. Cut each quesadilla into 4 wedges. Serve immediately with the salsa.

Note: This recipe can be turned into a quick canapé by cutting 2-inch (5-cm) rounds out of thinly sliced pumpernickel bread, piping on the cream cheese filling and topping with strips of smoked salmon and a sprig of dill. The filling is also delicious stuffed into hollowed-out cherry tomatoes or piped onto cucumber rounds.

Mango Grapefruit Salsa

Makes 1¹/₂ cups (360 mL)

This sweet salsa goes well with smoked fish, seafood dishes and grilled chicken. Substitute fresh basil or cilantro if chives are unavailable.

1	ripe mango, peeled and diced	1
1	grapefruit, peeled and diced	1
¹/₄ cup	finely chopped green onions	60 mL
1 Tbsp.	fresh lemon juice	15 mL
1	clove garlic, minced	1
1 Tbsp.	olive oil	15 mL
	salt and freshly ground black pepper to taste	
2 Tbsp.	chopped fresh chives	30 mL

Combine the mango, grapefruit, onion, lemon juice, garlic and olive oil. Season with salt and pepper. Cover and refrigerate for 30 minutes or up to 6 hours to blend the flavors. Sprinkle with the chives before serving.

About Mangos

Select a ripe but firm fruit with no blemishes. A ripe mango yields gently when pressed. The fruit will feel heavy and have a pleasant scent at the stem end. If the smell is sour, the fruit has begun to ferment and is overripe. Do not refrigerate mangos; leave them at room temperature in a cool place. To hasten ripening, place in a paper bag with a banana or apple.

To prepare a mango, slice it lengthwise into 2 pieces, cutting on either side of the long pit. This prevents cutting the fibrous center. Score the flesh of each half, making a crisscross pattern. Do not cut through the skin. Turn each mango inside out and cut off the pieces.

Rosemary Chicken Salad Wrap

Makes 32 pieces

Delicate tender pieces of shredded chicken are blended with mayonnaise and fresh rosemary and rolled into a soft tortilla. You can substitute your favorite sandwich filling for the chicken.

1 1/2 cups	cooked, shredded chicken breast	360 mL
1/2 cup	sliced green onions	120 mL
1/4 cup	chopped celery	60 mL
1/2 cup	mayonnaise	120 mL
1 Tbsp.	minced fresh rosemary, or 1 tsp. (5 mL) dried	15 mL
	salt and freshly ground black pepper to taste	
4	8-inch (20-cm) flour tortillas	4
1	red bell pepper, sliced into 12 strips	1
4	large lettuce leaves	4
2 Tbsp.	pine nuts, toasted	30 mL
	rosemary sprigs	

Combine the chicken, green onion and celery. Stir in the mayonnaise and rosemary. Season with salt and pepper.

Arrange the tortillas on your work surface. Spread the chicken mixture evenly over half of each tortilla. Place 3 strips of red pepper and 1 lettuce leaf over top of the mixture. Divide the pine nuts evenly among the tortillas. Roll each tortilla up tightly. Wrap in plastic wrap and refrigerate for at least 1 hour and up to 1 day.

Cut each tortilla into 8 1-inch (2.5-cm) slices. Secure with a toothpick. Place on a serving platter. Garnish with a sprig of rosemary, if desired. Serve chilled or at room temperature.

Casual Entertaining

An informal get-together to watch a sports game or play a round of cards calls for satisfying and hearty finger foods. Buffalo Chicken Wings, bite-size Reuben sandwiches and Fried Mozzarella Sticks are classic favorites.

The recipes in this chapter can be served in larger portions and are slightly more messy to eat. Make sure to provide plenty of napkins and plates. Guests will need to dispose of toothpicks, skewers and shells, so provide baskets or other containers to discreetly collect these items.

Create a comfortable and relaxing atmosphere for your guests by setting out baskets of delicious nibbles. Spiced Pecans, Spicy Honey-Roasted Peanuts and a Mexican Layer Salad allow guests to help themselves and feel right at home.

Choose recipes that can be served at room temperature, which allows you to spend more time with your guests and less time in the kitchen.

Moroccan Beef Kebabs

Makes approximately 32 skewers

1 lb.	sirloin steak	455 g
1 tsp.	ground cumin	5 mL
1/2 tsp.	cayenne	2.5 mL
1/2 tsp.	paprika	2.5 mL
1 tsp.	ground coriander	5 mL
1/2 tsp.	freshly ground black pepper	2.5 mL
1/4 cup	olive oil	60 mL
1/4 cup	red wine	60 mL
3	Japanese eggplants, cut into 1/2-inch (1.2-cm) cubes	3
	salt and freshly ground black pepper to taste	

Trim the sirloin of any excess fat. Cut it into 1-inch (2.5-cm) cubes.

Combine the cumin, cayenne, paprika, coriander and pepper in a large bowl. Add the meat and rub it with the spices. Add the olive oil and red wine. Toss well to coat. Cover and marinate up to 6 hours in the refrigerator.

One hour before barbecuing, soak 32 wooden skewers in cold water.

Thread 2 pieces of sirloin and 1 piece of eggplant onto the presoaked wooden skewers. Season with salt and pepper. Heat the barbecue or broiler to high and brush the grill or broiler pan with oil. Grill the kebabs 3–4 minutes on each side, brushing each side with the marinade before grilling. Serve immediately.

Rubbing the meat with a dry spice mixture before marinating allows the flavor of the spices to come through. Japanese eggplant is long, slender and deep purple. Choose an eggplant that feels heavy and has a smooth, firm skin. If you are unable to find Japanese eggplant, you can use regular eggplant. Salt it and place in a colander to drain for 30 minutes. Pat it dry with paper towels.

Chicken and Green Pepper Kebabs

Tender pieces of chicken are marinated in a teriyaki-style glaze and grilled to perfection with green pepper. The marinade can be made several days in advance and refrigerated.

Makes approximately 24 kebabs

1 cup	mirin, or rice wine (see page 151)	240 mL
1/2 cup	sugar	120 mL
3/4 cup	soy sauce	180 mL
1 tsp.	fresh minced ginger	5 mL
2	cloves garlic, minced	2
1 1/2 lbs.	boneless, skinless chicken breasts, cut into 1/2-inch (1.2-cm) pieces	680 g
2	large green peppers, cut into 1/2-inch (1.2-cm) pieces	2
2	sprigs cilantro	2

Soak 24 wooden skewers for 1 hour in cold water.

Combine the mirin, sugar, soy sauce, ginger and garlic in a small saucepan. Cook the mixture over medium-low heat until it is reduced by half and is syrupy. Remove from the heat and cool.

Ginger

Ginger is a rhizome with a light brown skin. Look for pieces that are juicy and pale yellow in color with a fresh scent when cut or snapped. Whether or not to peel ginger is a personal choice; I usually just wash it. Store it in a plastic bag in the refrigerator for about 1 week. For longer storage, peel it and place it in a jar and cover with rice vinegar. Use the vinegar to flavor stir-fries or as a salad dressing. Powdered ginger is used in baking and cannot be substituted for fresh ginger.

Place the chicken in a large non-reactive bowl and add the marinade; toss well. Cover and marinate in the refrigerator for 2 hours or up to 24 hours. Remove the chicken from the marinade and thread it on the presoaked skewers, alternating chicken and pepper pieces.

Heat the barbecue or broiler to high and brush the grill or broiler pan with oil. Grill the chicken 3–4 minutes on each side, or until it is no longer pink. Brush each side with the marinade before grilling. Place the kebabs on a serving platter. Garnish with the cilantro and serve immediately.

Chicken Saté with Spicy Peanut Sauce

Makes approximately 24 pieces

Indonesian saté is thinly sliced, tender strips of chicken, beef or pork, grilled quickly over an open flame. It is traditionally served with a spicy sauce and sprinkled with chopped peanuts.

1/2 cup	unsweetened coconut milk	120 mL
2 Tbsp.	soy sauce	30 mL
2 Tbsp.	rice vinegar	30 mL
1 Tbsp.	brown sugar	15 mL
1 tsp.	curry powder	5 mL
1 tsp.	ground turmeric	5 mL
2	cloves garlic, minced	2
1 1/2 lbs.	boneless, skinless chicken breast	680 g
1/4 cup	thinly sliced green onions	60 mL
2 Tbsp.	chopped unsalted peanuts	30 mL
1 recipe	Spicy Peanut Sauce	1 recipe

Combine the coconut milk, soy sauce, rice vinegar, brown sugar, curry powder, turmeric and garlic in a large bowl. Set aside.

Wash the chicken and pat it dry. Cut it into 1/2-inch (1.2-cm) strips. Add the chicken to the coconut milk mixture and toss well. Cover and marinate 2 hours in the refrigerator. Soak 1 wooden skewer for each chicken strip in cold water for 1 hour.

Thread one strip of chicken onto the presoaked wooden skewer. Heat the barbecue or broiler to high and brush the grill or broiler pan with oil. Grill the chicken 3–4 minutes on each side, or until it's no longer pink, brushing each side with marinade before grilling. Place the skewers on a serving platter and sprinkle with green onions and chopped peanuts. Serve with the peanut sauce.

Spicy Peanut Sauce

Makes 1 cup (240 mL)

This Thai-inspired sauce makes a great dip for chicken, beef and pork saté and raw vegetables. If the dip is too thick, thin it with a little warm water or chicken stock. For a creamier dip, purchase a smooth, natural peanut butter, available at health food stores and some supermarkets. If you like, you can make the dip fiery hot by adding more sambal oelek.

1/2 cup	peanut butter	120 mL
2 Tbsp.	soy sauce	30 mL
2	cloves garlic, minced	2
1 Tbsp.	honey	15 mL
2 Tbsp.	fresh lemon juice	30 mL
2 tsp.	sambal oelek (see page 64)	10 mL
1/4 cup	unsweetened coconut milk	60 mL
2 Tbsp.	chopped fresh cilantro	30 mL

Combine the peanut butter, soy sauce, garlic, honey, lemon juice and sambal oelek. Add the coconut milk and blend until smooth. Transfer to a serving bowl and sprinkle with the chopped cilantro. Serve warm or at room temperature.

The sauce can be stored in an airtight container in the refrigerator for 3 days and brought back to room temperature before serving.

Coconut Milk

Coconut milk has a slightly sweet, rich flavor. It is sold in cans or glass jars. Look for Chaokoh or Chef's Choice, both from Thailand. The thick top layer is sometimes referred to as coconut cream or thick milk. Make sure the liquid bottom half and the coconut cream are stirred together before using it in recipes. Pour any leftovers into a glass jar and refrigerate for up to 1 week.

Coconut Chicken and Pineapple Kebabs

Makes approximately 20 skewers

Bite-size meatballs are placed on skewers and grilled with chunks of juicy, ripe pineapple for a Polynesian flavor. Dark molasses and unsweetened coconut give this appetizer just the right amount of sweetness. For a dramatic buffet presentation, trim 1 inch (2.5 cm) off the base of a whole pineapple and stand it on a plate. Stud the grilled skewers around the pineapple.

1/2 lb.	lean ground chicken	225 g
1/4 cup	shredded unsweetened coconut	60 mL
2 Tbsp.	dark soy sauce	30 mL
2 Tbsp.	molasses	30 mL
2 tsp.	grated fresh ginger	10 mL
1 tsp.	fresh lime juice	5 mL
1/2 tsp.	salt	2.5 mL
1/2 tsp.	ground turmeric	2.5 mL
1/2 tsp.	ground cumin	2.5 mL
1/2 tsp.	freshly ground black pepper	2.5 mL
1	10-oz. (284-mL) can pineapple chunks, drained	1
2 Tbsp.	shredded unsweetened coconut	30 mL

Soak 24 wooden skewers for 1 hour in cold water.

Combine the ground chicken, 1/4 cup (60 mL) coconut, soy sauce, molasses, ginger, lime juice, salt, turmeric, cumin and pepper in a large bowl. Mix well.

Shape the mixture into 1-inch (2.5-cm) balls. Thread 2 meatballs and 1 chunk of pineapple on each wooden skewer.

Heat the barbecue or broiler to high and brush the grill or broiler pan with oil. Cook the kebabs for 3 minutes on each side or until the meat is no longer pink. Arrange the kebabs on a serving platter and sprinkle with shredded coconut. Serve hot.

Sesame Honey Chicken Drumettes

Makes 24 pieces

1/2 cup	honey	120 mL
2 Tbsp.	Dijon mustard	30 mL
1 Tbsp.	soy sauce	15 mL
1 Tbsp.	rice vinegar	15 mL
1 tsp.	hot chili flakes	5 mL
24	chicken drumettes	24
1 tsp.	salt	5 mL
1/2 tsp.	freshly ground black pepper	2.5 mL
1 Tbsp.	sesame seeds, toasted	15 mL

These honey-glazed chicken drumettes are so addictive that you will have a hard time keeping the platter full. Toasting the sesame seeds in a dry frying pan over low heat for 2–3 minutes brings out their nutty flavor and golden color.

Preheat the oven to 375°F (190°C).

Combine the honey, mustard, soy sauce, rice vinegar and chili flakes in a small bowl. Set aside.

Rinse the drumettes under cold water and pat dry. Place them in a roasting pan and sprinkle with salt and pepper. Bake, uncovered, for 40 minutes, turning after 20 minutes. Remove from the heat and discard the fat and liquid.

Pour the honey mustard sauce over the drumettes and toss well. Return to the oven. Bake until the chicken is crispy and golden in color, about 30 to 40 minutes. Transfer to a serving platter, sprinkle with sesame seeds and serve immediately.

Sesame Seeds

White sesame seeds are available in the spice section of your local supermarket. To prevent them from becoming rancid, store in an airtight container in the freezer for up to 6 months.

Buffalo Chicken Wings

Makes 24 pieces

These spicy chicken morsels originated in Buffalo, New York, and have been a hit ever since. Serve them with Creamy Blue Cheese Dip (page 22) and crisp celery sticks to temper the heat.

12	chicken wings	12
2 Tbsp.	melted butter	30 mL
1/2 tsp.	paprika	2.5 mL
1/2 tsp.	freshly ground black pepper	2.5 mL
1/2 tsp.	salt	2.5 mL
1 Tbsp.	hot sauce	15 mL

Preheat the oven to 400°F (200°C).

Rinse the chicken wings and pat them dry. Cut off the wing tips. Cut the wings at the joint to form 24 pieces.

Combine the butter, paprika, pepper, salt and hot sauce in a large bowl. Add the wing pieces and toss to coat.

Arrange the wings on a metal rack placed over a baking sheet. Bake for 15 minutes per side or until golden and crisp. Transfer the wings to a serving platter and serve hot.

Facing page: *Tomato Basil Bruschetta (p. 101)*.

Following page: *Rosemary and Onion Focaccia (p. 102)*.

Grilled Italian Sausage Bites with Hot Honey-Mustard Sauce

Makes 12 pieces

| 1 lb. | Italian veal and pork sausage | 455 g |
| 1 recipe | Hot Honey-Mustard Sauce | 1 recipe |

With a fork, prick the sausage in several places. Place on a preheated barbecue. Cook for 5 minutes on each side or until it's no longer pink. Remove from the heat.

Slice the sausage diagonally into ½ inch (1.2-cm) pieces. Thread each piece onto a decorative toothpick. Serve hot with the sauce.

I like to serve these juicy, spicy sausages with Hot Honey Mustard Sauce and crusty French bread. Polish kielbasa or Mexican chorizo may be substituted for the Italian sausage, and all are available at your local supermarket or ethnic market.

Hot Honey-Mustard Sauce

Makes ½ cup (120 mL)

Here is the perfect sauce to jazz up grilled sausage and chicken fingers. A store-bought honey mustard can be used if you are short on time.

¼ cup	cider vinegar	60 mL
¼ cup	honey	60 mL
1 Tbsp.	brown sugar	15 mL
¼ cup	dry mustard powder	60 mL
1 tsp.	all-purpose flour	5 mL
¼ tsp.	hot sauce	1.2 mL
⅛ tsp.	salt	.5 mL

Combine the vinegar, honey and brown sugar in a small saucepan. Cook over medium-low heat for 1 minute. Remove from the heat. Add the mustard, flour and hot sauce. Season with salt. Return to the heat and cook for 1 minute, whisking constantly. Cool before serving.

The sauce can be stored in an airtight container in the refrigerator for 1 month.

Maple-Glazed Baby Back Ribs

These sweet, succulent baby back ribs are roasted to perfection and brushed with a maple syrup glaze. You can substitute honey for the maple syrup.

Makes 12 servings

3 lbs.	pork baby back ribs	1.4 kg
1/4 cup	pure maple syrup	60 mL
1/4 cup	apricot preserves	60 mL
2 Tbsp.	brown sugar	30 ml
1 Tbsp.	soy sauce	15 mL
2 Tbsp.	rice vinegar	30 mL
1/2 tsp.	salt	2.5 mL
1/8 tsp.	freshly ground black pepper	.5 mL

Preheat the oven to 350ºF (175ºC).

Cut the ribs between the bones. Arrange them in a single layer on a metal rack over a baking sheet. Bake for 1 hour. Drain off the fat.

Combine the maple syrup, apricot preserves, brown sugar, soy sauce, rice vinegar, salt and pepper in a small saucepan. Bring to a boil. Reduce the heat and cook the mixture for 2 minutes.

Brush the ribs with the glaze. Return them to the oven and bake 20–25 minutes, basting occasionally with the glaze. Place on a serving platter. Serve hot.

Swedish Meatballs

Makes approximately 70 meatballs

A retro dish from the '50s that has been lightened up for today's taste.

1 lb.	lean ground beef	455 g
1/2 cup	dry bread crumbs	120 mL
1/4 cup	milk	60 mL
1	egg, slightly beaten	1
1/2 tsp.	paprika	2.5 mL
1 tsp.	salt	5 mL
1 Tbsp.	Worcestershire sauce	15 mL
2 Tbsp.	vegetable oil	30 mL
4 Tbsp.	all-purpose flour	60 mL
2 cups	half-and-half cream	475 mL
	salt and freshly ground pepper to taste	
1 Tbsp.	chopped fresh dill	15 mL

In a large bowl, combine the beef, bread crumbs, milk, egg, paprika, salt and Worcestershire sauce. Shape the mixture into 1-inch (2.5-cm) balls.

Heat 1 Tbsp. (15 mL) of the oil in a large non-stick frying pan over medium-high heat. Cook the meatballs for 3 minutes per side, or until the centers are cooked. Drain on paper towels. Add more oil if necessary. Repeat with the remaining meatballs.

Blend the flour into the pan drippings and cook over low heat for 3 minutes. Gradually whisk in the cream. Bring to a boil. Lower the heat and continue to cook for 5 minutes, or until the sauce coats the back of a spoon. Season with salt and pepper. Return the meatballs to the pan and heat through. Transfer to a serving dish, sprinkle with the dill and serve warm with toothpicks.

Honey-Glazed Meatballs with Sweet and Sour Glaze

Makes about 70 meatballs

These easily prepared meatballs can be served as an appetizer or a substantial main course. Just accompany them with fresh bread and a crisp, light salad.

1 lb.	lean ground beef	455 g
2	cloves garlic, minced	2
2 Tbsp.	chopped fresh parsley	30 mL
1 Tbsp.	Worcestershire sauce	15 mL
3 Tbsp.	fresh bread crumbs	45 mL
1	egg, slightly beaten	1
1/2 tsp.	salt	2.5 mL
1/4 tsp.	freshly ground black pepper	1.2 mL
1 Tbsp.	vegetable oil	15 mL
1 recipe	Sweet and Sour Glaze	1 recipe

Combine the ground beef, garlic, parsley, Worcestershire sauce, bread crumbs, egg, salt and pepper. Mix well and shape into 1-inch (2.5-cm) balls.

Preheat the oven to 350°F (175°C).

Heat the oil in a large non-stick frying pan over medium-high heat. Cook the meatballs in 2 batches for 3 minutes per side, or until the center is cooked. Drain on paper towels. Add more oil if necessary. The meatballs can be prepared in advance and frozen in an airtight container for up to 1 month.

Place the meatballs in a large casserole dish and cover with the sweet and sour glaze. Bake for 15 minutes. Serve with toothpicks or small skewers.

Sweet and Sour Glaze

Makes 1/2 cup (120 mL)

This sweet glaze can be used as a sauce with cocktail meatballs or a dipping sauce for fried foods.

1/4 cup	brown sugar	60 mL
1/4 cup	plum sauce	60 mL
2 Tbsp.	rice vinegar	30 mL
1 tsp.	minced ginger	5 mL
1/4 cup	pineapple juice	60 mL
1 Tbsp.	ketchup	15 mL
1 tsp.	cornstarch	5 mL

Combine all the ingredients in a small saucepan. Cook over medium-low heat for 5 minutes, or until slightly thickened.

The sauce can be stored in an airtight container in the refrigerator for 3 days and warmed before serving.

Coconut Macadamia Chicken Strips with Raspberry Mustard Sauce

These moist, crunchy chicken strips make a fabulous appetizer. I have reduced the fat by baking them in the oven.

Makes 12 pieces

1/2 tsp.	cayenne	2.5 mL
1/4 tsp.	paprika	1.2 mL
1/4 tsp.	freshly ground black pepper	1.2 mL
1/4 tsp.	salt	1.2 mL
2	cloves garlic, minced	2
3	4-oz. (113-g) skinless, boneless chicken breasts	3
2	large eggs	2
1/2 cup	shredded unsweetened coconut	120 mL
1/2 cup	macadamia nuts, toasted and finely chopped	120 mL
1 recipe	Raspberry Mustard Sauce	1 recipe

Preheat the oven to 375°F (190°C).

Combine the cayenne, paprika, black pepper, salt and garlic in a medium bowl.

Slice the chicken into 1/2-inch (1.2-cm) strips. Toss the chicken with the spices, making sure it's well coated.

In a small bowl, beat the eggs. Combine the shredded coconut and macadamia nuts in a shallow dish. Dip the chicken strips into the beaten egg, then roll them in the coconut mixture to coat all sides and shake off the excess. The chicken can be made to this point 1 day in advance, covered and stored in the refrigerator.

Place the chicken on a lightly greased baking sheet. Bake for 12–15 minutes, or until crispy and golden brown. Serve with the sauce on the side.

Raspberry Mustard Sauce

Makes 1 cup (240 mL)

This sauce is quick to make and calls for ingredients you have on hand. Try it as a spread with roast turkey or grilled chicken and sliced tart apples. It will keep in the refrigerator for up to 3 weeks.

1/2 cup	raspberry jam	120 mL
1/4 cup	honey	60 mL
2 Tbsp.	Dijon mustard	30 mL
1/2 tsp.	cayenne pepper	2.5 mL
1 Tbsp.	fresh lemon juice	15 mL
1/4 tsp.	freshly ground pepper	1.2 mL

Combine all the ingredients. Cover and chill until serving time.

Fried Calamari with Quick Lemon Aïoli Sauce

Makes 8 servings

These tender golden rings are a treat to eat and can be served with the lemon aïoli or Cocktail Sauce (page 34). Cleaned small squid is available in the frozen section of your local supermarket or any ethnic market. Thaw in the refrigerator overnight or soak in cold water at room temperature for 30 minutes.

2 lbs.	cleaned squid	900 g
2 cups	all-purpose flour	475 mL
1/2 tsp.	salt	2.5 mL
1/4 tsp.	freshly ground black pepper	1.2 mL
2 Tbsp.	chopped fresh parsley	30 mL
1 recipe	Quick Lemon Aïoli Sauce	1 recipe

Slice the squid into 1/2-inch (1.2-cm) rings. Place in a colander and rinse well. (The squid can be stored in an airtight container in the refrigerator for 1 day. Add 2 cups (475 mL) milk to the container to soften the squid and maintain the white color.)

Heat 1 inch (2.5 cm) of vegetable oil in a wok or deep pot over medium-high to 375°F (190°C).

Combine the flour, salt and pepper in a bowl. Dredge a few squid rings at a time in the flour. Remove and shake off the excess flour. Don't let the squid pieces sit too long in the flour or they will become gummy and stick together.

Working in small batches, drop the squid into the hot oil. Cook for 1 minute, or until just barely golden. Do not overcook or they will become chewy rather than tender. Transfer the squid with a slotted spoon onto paper towels to drain. Repeat with the remaining squid. Arrange on a serving platter and sprinkle with the parsley. Serve immediately with the aïoli sauce.

Quick Lemon Aïoli Sauce

Makes ½ cup (120 mL)

This garlicky lemon mayonnaise is a popular condiment throughout the south of France. It is a perfect dipping sauce for crispy calamari or blanched vegetable crudités. Leftover sauce can be spooned onto steamed new potatoes or drizzled over poached salmon.

½ cup	mayonnaise	120 mL
1 Tbsp.	fresh lemon juice	15 mL
3	cloves garlic, pressed	3
¼ tsp.	cayenne pepper	1.2 mL
	salt and freshly ground pepper to taste	
1 tsp.	chopped fresh parsley	5 mL

Whisk together the mayonnaise, lemon juice, garlic and cayenne in a small bowl. Season with salt and pepper. Transfer to a serving bowl and sprinkle with the chopped parsley. Cover and chill.

The sauce can be stored in an airtight container in the refrigerator for 5 days.

Chicken Tostaditas with Black Bean and Corn Salsa

Makes 36 pieces

Tostaditas are round, bite-size tortilla chips topped with assorted fillings. Serve them with sour cream and the Black Bean and Corn Salsa here. You can substitute Salsa Cruda or use a store-bought salsa if time is short.

1/2 tsp.	salt	2.5 mL
1	bay leaf	1
1	onion, coarsely chopped	1
6	whole black peppercorns	6
2	4-oz (113-g) boneless, skinless chicken breasts	2
2 Tbsp.	olive oil	30 mL
1	small onion, finely chopped	1
2	cloves garlic, minced	2
1	large red bell pepper, finely chopped	1
1/4 cup	tomato-based salsa, such as Salsa Cruda (page 20)	60 mL
1 tsp.	ground cumin	5 mL
1/2 tsp.	salt	2.5 mL
1/4 tsp.	freshly ground black pepper	1.2 mL
36	round corn tortilla chips	36
1/2 cup	Black Bean and Corn Salsa	120 mL

Place the salt, bay leaf, onion and peppercorns in a medium pot of water and bring to a boil. Add the chicken, reduce the heat and cook for 12 to 15 minutes or until the chicken is no longer pink. Skim off any foam that rises to the top. Remove the chicken and let cool. Slice the chicken finely with a knife, or shred it. Set aside.

Heat the olive oil in a large frying pan over medium heat. Add the onion and garlic and cook until tender and fragrant. Add the red pepper and cook for 3 minutes, or until soft. Add the salsa and cumin and bring to a boil. Mix in the chicken. Season with salt and pepper. Remove from the heat.

Preheat the oven to 350ºF (175ºC). Arrange the tortilla chips on a baking sheet. Place a spoonful of the chicken mixture on each chip, and top with bean salsa. Bake for 7–8 minutes or until heated through. Transfer to a platter and serve hot.

Black Bean and Corn Salsa

Makes 3 cups (720 mL)

Using canned black beans cuts down on the preparation time of this versatile salsa. Leftovers are great with tortilla chips and frosty mugs of beer. You can spread it on tortillas, top with shredded lettuce and cheese and roll up for a healthy lunch or simply add leftover salsa to soup.

1	14-oz (398-mL) can black beans, drained and rinsed	1
2	small tomatoes, seeded and chopped	2
1	small onion, diced	1
1/2 cup	frozen corn, thawed	120 mL
1	green pepper, chopped	1
1/4 cup	chopped fresh cilantro	60 mL
2	cloves garlic, minced	2
1 tsp.	ground cumin	5 mL
1/2 cup	vegetable oil	120 mL
2 Tbsp.	red wine vinegar	30 mL
1/2 tsp.	salt	2.5 mL
1/2 tsp.	freshly ground black pepper	2.5 mL

Combine all the ingredients. Cover and refrigerate 2 hours to allow the flavors to blend before serving.

The salsa can be stored in an airtight container in the refrigerator for 2 days.

Nachos

Makes 6 servings

Nachos are the perfect party food for a large group of hungry guests. If you like, serve them with smooth Guacamole (page 15) and Black Bean and Corn Salsa (page 93). Canned green chilies are pickled mild jalapeño chilies. They are sold in small jars or cans in the Mexican section of your local supermarket.

4 cups	corn tortilla chips	950 mL
1 1/2 cups	grated Cheddar cheese	360 mL
1	large tomato, chopped	1
2 Tbsp.	chopped, canned green chilies	30 mL
1/2 cup	light sour cream	120 mL

Preheat the oven to 350ºF (175ºC).

Spread the tortilla chips on a large ovenproof baking dish. Sprinkle with the grated cheese, tomato and chopped green chilies. Bake for 3 to 5 minutes, until the cheese melts and the chips are brown. Serve with sour cream on the side.

Mexican Layer Salad

Makes 6 servings

An all-time favorite dip that can be served hot or cold with a basket of tortilla chips.

1	14-oz. (398-mL) can refried beans	1
1 recipe	Guacamole (page 15)	1 recipe
1 cup	sour cream	240 mL
1/2 cup	chopped tomatoes	120 mL
1/4 cup	chopped green onions	60 mL
1/4 cup	chopped pitted olives	60 mL
1 cup	grated Cheddar cheese	240 mL
2 Tbsp.	chopped fresh cilantro or parsley	30 mL

Spread the bottom of a 9-inch (23-cm), 1 1/2-inch-deep (3.8-cm) serving dish with the refried beans. Top with a layer of guacamole, then sour cream.

Garnish with concentric rings of chopped tomatoes on the outside, then green onions and the olives and cheese in the center. Sprinkle with the parsley or cilantro.

Serve cold or heat in a 400°F (200°C) oven for 15 minutes. The spread can be made 12 hours in advance, stored in a covered container and warmed before serving.

Pizzettas

Makes approximately 26

These bite-size pizzas can be topped with an assortment of vegetables, cheeses and herbs. If you are too busy to prepare the dough, go ahead and use store-bought frozen bread dough.

1/2 recipe	Pizza Dough (page 161)	1/2 recipe
1/2 cup	Fresh Tomato Sauce (page 169)	120 mL
1 cup	grated mozzarella cheese	240 mL

Preheat the oven to 375°F (190°C).

Punch the dough down and knead it for 3 minutes. Divide the dough into 26 2-inch (5-cm) balls. On a lightly floured surface, roll each ball into a 3-inch (7.5-cm) round. Place the rounds on a lightly greased baking sheet. Spread tomato sauce over each round and sprinkle with grated cheese. Bake for 8 minutes or until crispy. Serve hot or cold.

For a change, try any of the quick toppings below:

▸ Fresh fontina, sliced tomato and chopped fresh basil

▸ Caramelized onions

▸ Anchovies, olives and capers

▸ Eggplant, roasted red peppers and sun-dried tomatoes

▸ Asiago cheese and salsa

▸ Romano cheese and pesto

Mini Reubens

Makes 24 pieces

24	slices cocktail-size rye bread	24	
2 Tbsp.	butter, softened	30 mL	
1/4 cup	Dijon mustard	60 mL	
2 oz.	corned beef, thinly sliced	57 g	
1/2 cup	sauerkraut, drained and chopped	120 mL	
1/2 cup	grated Swiss cheese	120 mL	
2 Tbsp.	butter	30 mL	

These tiny grilled sandwiches are wonderful served with Pesto (page 168).

Butter one side of each slice of rye bread. Spread the mustard evenly on 12 slices of bread. Layer the corned beef, sauerkraut and Swiss cheese on the mustard. Top with the remaining slices, buttered side out.

Melt the remaining 2 Tbsp. (30 mL) butter in a large non-stick frying pan over medium-high heat. Place the sandwiches buttered side up in the frying pan and cook in small batches until the cheese melts and they are crispy on one side (about 1 minute). Turn the sandwiches over and brown the other side. Transfer to a platter and serve hot.

Fried Mozzarella Sticks

Makes 20 pieces

These irresistible tidbits are delicious served on their own or with Fresh Tomato Sauce (page 169). Try to purchase a high-quality fresh mozzarella, available at your local supermarket.

1/2 lb.	mozzarella cheese	225 g
2	eggs	2
1/2 tsp.	salt	2.5 mL
1/4 tsp.	freshly grated black pepper	1.2 mL
2 cups	fine dry bread crumbs	475 mL
1 tsp.	chopped fresh parsley	5 mL
1 Tbsp.	freshly grated Parmesan Cheese	30 mL

Cut the mozzarella cheese into 1/4-inch (.6-cm) sticks.

In a small bowl, beat together the eggs, salt and pepper. Combine the bread crumbs, parsley and Parmesan cheese in a shallow bowl. Dip the cheese sticks into the egg mixture, then roll them in the bread crumbs. Press the crumbs firmly onto the cheese sticks. Place them on a platter until you're ready to fry them.

Heat 1/2 inch (1.2 cm) vegetable oil in a large frying pan over medium-high heat. Cook the cheese sticks for 3 minutes on both sides, or until they're golden brown. Drain on paper towels. Arrange the mozzarella sticks on a platter and serve warm.

The mozzarella sticks can be made ahead of time and reheated in a 350ºF (175ºC) oven for 7 minutes.

Facing page: *Marinated Vegetables (p. 111).*

Parmesan Cheese Straws

Makes approximately 36

¹/2 cup	grated Parmesan cheese	60 mL
2 Tbsp.	chopped fresh parsley	30 mL
1	1-lb. (455-g) package frozen puff pastry, thawed	1
1	egg, beaten	1

Preheat the oven to 400°F (200°C).

Combine the Parmesan cheese and parsley. Line a baking sheet with parchment paper or a brown paper bag.

On a lightly floured surface, roll the puff pastry dough into a 15- by 10-inch (38- by 25-cm) rectangle. Brush the beaten egg over the pastry and sprinkle with the cheese mixture. Using a sharp knife, cut the pastry into ¹/2-inch (1.2-cm) strips. Gently twist each strip into a straw.

Place the strips on the prepared baking sheet. Bake about 10 minutes, or until puffed and golden brown. Serve warm or at room temperature.

These crispy, flaky cheese straws can be topped with grated Romano or Asiago cheese instead of Parmesan. Ready-made puff pastry is available in the frozen section of your local supermarket. Thaw the pastry in the refrigerator for several hours before using it.

Facing page: *Spiced Pecans (p. 113) and Spicy Honey-Roasted Peanuts (p. 112)*

Mushroom Tarts

Makes 16 tarts

You can use a variety of fresh cultivated mushrooms available at your local super-market. Shiitake, crimini, portobello or chanterelle mushrooms work well in this recipe. Use light cream cheese instead of regular for a low-fat alternative.

1/4 cup	butter	60 mL
1	small onion, finely chopped	1
4 cups	mushrooms, sliced	950 mL
1 Tbsp.	dry white wine	15 mL
1	4-oz. (113-g) package cream cheese, softened	1
1 tsp.	chopped fresh rosemary, or 1/2 tsp. (2.5 mL) dried	5 mL
4	slices cooked bacon, crumbled	4
	salt and black pepper to taste	
16	Bread Cups (page 160)	16
1 Tbsp.	chopped fresh dill	15 mL

Melt the butter in a large frying pan over medium-high heat. Add the onion and cook until tender and fragrant, about 7 minutes. Add the mushrooms and white wine. Cook for 4 minutes, or until the mushrooms are soft and half the liquid has evaporated. Stir in the cream cheese, rosemary and bacon. Season with salt and pepper. Set the mixture aside to cool.

Preheat the oven to 350°F (175°C).

Divide the mushroom mixture equally among the 16 bread cups. Arrange the cups on a baking sheet. Bake for 7 minutes, or until the cheese is bubbly. Transfer to a platter, sprinkle with chopped dill and serve immediately.

Tomato Basil Bruschetta

Makes 24 pieces

4	medium tomatoes, seeded and diced	4
1/4 cup	extra-virgin olive oil	60 mL
1/4 cup	finely chopped fresh basil	60 mL
1 tsp.	salt	5 mL
	freshly ground black pepper to taste	
24	slices French bread, 2 inches (5 cm) in diameter and 1/2 inch (1.2 cm) thick	24
2	cloves garlic, crushed	2
1/4 cup	freshly grated Parmesan cheese	60 mL
2 Tbsp.	chopped fresh parsley	30 mL

In a small bowl, combine the tomatoes, olive oil and basil. Season with salt and pepper. Cover and let stand at room temperature for 1 hour before serving in order to allow the flavors to blend.

Brush one side of the bread lightly with oil and rub with the garlic. Grill or broil the bread lightly on both sides until golden brown. Top each slice with a generous spoonful of the tomato mixture and sprinkle with Parmesan cheese. Garnish with parsley. Serve at room temperature.

This bruschetta is a simple, delicious appetizer, using thick slices of country bread. I like to make it in the summer using the ripest, most luscious and fragrant tomatoes from my garden. The topping should be at room temperature and the bruschetta assembled no more than 30 minutes before serving, or the bread will become soggy.

Rosemary and Onion Focaccia

Makes approximately 24 pieces

Focaccia is a savory flatbread topped with fresh herbs and assorted cooked vegetables. Cooking the onions on low heat will result in a golden onion topping.

1 recipe	Pizza Dough (page 161)	1 recipe
6 Tbsp.	olive oil	90 mL
1/2 tsp.	salt	2.5 mL
3	large onions, sliced thinly	3
1 tsp.	sugar	5 mL
1/2 tsp.	salt	2.5 mL
1 Tbsp.	chopped fresh rosemary	15 mL
1/2 cup	freshly grated Parmesan cheese	120 mL

Make the pizza dough and when it has risen, punch it down. Turn the dough out onto a lightly floured surface and knead for 2 minutes. Roll or press the dough to fit an oiled baking sheet. Cover with a tea towel and let rise for 45 minutes.

When the dough has risen, dimple the top with your fingers. Brush with 3 Tbsp. (45 mL) of the olive oil and sprinkle with salt. Set aside.

Heat the remaining 3 Tbsp. (45 mL) of olive oil in a large non-stick skillet over low heat. Add the onions, sugar, salt and rosemary. Cook for 30 minutes, stirring occasionally, until the onions are tender and lightly brown. Cool to room temperature.

Preheat the oven to 350°F (175°C).

Spread the onions evenly over the dough. Sprinkle with the Parmesan cheese. Bake for 20–25 minutes, until the bottom is crisp. Cut into 2-inch (5-cm) wedges and arrange on a platter. Serve warm or at room temperature.

Zucchini Pakoras

Makes 36 pieces

2	small zucchini	2	
1/2 tsp.	salt	2.5 mL	
1 cup	chickpea flour	240 mL	
1/2 tsp.	salt	2.5 mL	
1 tsp.	ground cumin	5 mL	
1/4 tsp.	freshly ground black pepper	1.2 mL	
1/2 tsp.	cayenne	2.5 mL	
1/2 tsp.	ground coriander	2.5 mL	
1 tsp.	baking powder	5 mL	
3/4 cup	cold water	180 mL	
1 recipe	Tzatziki (page 13)	1 recipe	

Pakoras are little vegetable pieces dipped in a ground chickpea batter and fried quickly. You can use other vegetables, such as onions, thinly sliced potatoes and eggplant, to produce these tender fritters. Chickpea flour is also called besan flour and is available at East Indian grocery stores or health food stores.

Trim off the ends of the zucchini. Slice crosswise into 1/4-inch (.6-cm) rounds. Place in a glass bowl and sprinkle with 1/2 tsp. (2.5 mL) salt. Toss gently and allow to sit no longer than 5 minutes. Pat dry with paper towels.

In a large bowl, combine the chickpea flour, the remaining 1/2 tsp. (2.5 mL) salt, cumin, pepper, cayenne, coriander and baking powder. Slowly whisk in the cold water until the batter is smooth.

Heat 1 inch (2.5 cm) vegetable oil in a wok or large frying pan over medium-high heat. Dip several zucchini slices into the batter. Remove with tongs and drop gently into the hot oil. Cook for 1 minute per side, or until golden brown. Drain on paper towels. Repeat with the remaining zucchini, adding more oil if necessary. Place on a warm serving platter. Serve immediately with the tzatziki.

Pakoras can be fried ahead of time and reheated on a baking sheet lined with parchment paper at 400°F (200°C) for 4 minutes.

Frittata

Makes 8–10 servings

2 Tbsp.	olive oil	30 mL
1	medium onion, sliced	1
2	medium zucchini, thinly sliced	2
10	large eggs	10
2 Tbsp.	chopped fresh parsley	30 mL
1 Tbsp.	chopped fresh basil	15 mL
1/2 tsp.	salt	2.5 mL
1/4 tsp.	freshly ground black pepper	1.2 mL

In my home, frittatas are a weekly luncheon dish. They are wonderful hot or cold, or tucked into foccacia or any other bread. You can add a variety of fresh herbs, vegetables or meats to this base recipe. For an elegant presentation, cut out circles with a cookie cutter and use the leftover trims chopped into a salad.

Heat 1 Tbsp. (15 mL) of the oil in a large, non-stick, ovenproof frying pan. Add the onion and cook until tender. Add the zucchini and cook 5 minutes.

Preheat the oven to 350°F (175°C).

In a large bowl, beat the eggs, parsley, basil, salt and pepper. Blend in the onion and zucchini mixture. Heat the remaining 1 Tbsp. (15 mL) oil in the same skillet. Add the egg mixture and cook over medium heat until partially set. Lift the edges of the frittata to let the egg mixture run underneath. Remove from the heat.

Place in the oven and bake an additional 10 minutes, or until the center is set. Let cool. With a spatula, carefully lift the frittata onto a cutting board. Slice into small wedges or cut into rounds. Serve hot or at room temperature.

Devilled Eggs

Makes 16 pieces

8	large hard-boiled eggs	8	
1/2 cup	mayonnaise	120 mL	
1 tsp.	Dijon mustard	5 mL	
1/4 tsp.	salt	1.2 mL	
1 tsp.	chili paste	5 mL	
1/4 tsp.	freshly ground black pepper	1.2 mL	
	paprika		

Peel the eggs and cut them in half lengthwise. Remove the yolks and place in a small bowl. Once the eggs are halved, cut a small slice off the base to prevent the eggs from rolling around on the platter.

Process the egg yolks, mayonnaise, mustard, salt, chili paste and pepper in a blender or food processor until smooth and creamy. Using a pastry bag or a small spoon, fill the egg white halves with the yolk mixture.

Arrange them on a serving platter and sprinkle with paprika. Serve chilled or at room temperature.

Curried Eggs: Add 1/2 tsp. (2.5 mL) curry powder and 1/4 tsp. (1.2 mL) ground turmeric.
Herbed Eggs: Add 1/4 tsp. (1.2 mL) each finely chopped chervil, tarragon, thyme and marjoram.

I have spiced this old-time favorite with just the right amount of chili paste. The egg yolk filling can be made a day in advance and refrigerated in an airtight container. Use only fresh eggs and add a drop of lemon juice to the filling to prevent discoloration of the yolk. Do not assemble the devilled eggs more than 2 hours prior to serving or they will discolor. Chili paste is available in Chinese markets and many large supermarkets.

Stuffed Jalapeños

These miniature cheese-stuffed jalapeños pack a lot of heat. Removing the seeds and white rib from these thick green chilies before roasting will make them milder.

Makes 12 pieces

12	fresh jalapeño chilies	12
2	eggs, slightly beaten	2
1/4 tsp.	salt	1.2 mL
1/8 tsp.	pepper	.5 mL
1/2 cup	bread crumbs	120 mL
1	4-oz. (113-g) package cream cheese, softened	1
1 tsp.	fresh lemon juice	5 mL
1	clove garlic, minced	1
1/2 tsp.	ground cumin	2.5 mL
1/2 cup	sour cream	120 mL

Preheat the oven to 350ºF (175ºC).

Wash the chilies and pat them dry. With a sharp knife, remove the stems and cut the chilies in half. Scrape out the seeds and cut away the white membrane.

Working with Fresh Chili Peppers

To lessen the heat of chilies, remove the seeds and white rib with a sharp, small knife.

To protect sensitive skin, wear plastic gloves and do not touch your eyes or face. The chilies contain capsaicin, which can irritate or burn. Be sure to wash your hands with hot soapy water afterwards. (Tip: Rub your hands with oil to prevent your skin from becoming irritated if you're not wearing gloves.)

Place the chilies on a baking sheet and bake for 10 minutes, or until slightly soft. Remove from the oven and cool. With a knife, peel off the skin and discard it.

In a small bowl, beat together the eggs, salt and pepper. Place the bread crumbs in a shallow bowl. In another small bowl, combine the cream cheese, lemon juice, garlic and cumin. Spoon the cheese mixture on half the chilies. Place the remaining halves on top to form whole chilies. Dip each jalapeño into the egg mixture, then roll it in the bread crumbs.

Heat 1/2 inch (1.2 cm) oil in a large frying pan over medium-high heat. Cook the chilies for 1 minute per side, or until crisp and golden. Drain on paper towels. Serve warm with sour cream.

Sweet Potato Chips

Makes approximately 6 dozen

These crunchy, thin sweet potato chips are wonderful as a snack by themselves or dipped in a variety of sauces. Sweet potatoes are prone to bruising and rapid spoilage. Select firm potatoes with no large brown spots. Store them in a well-ventilated area for up to a week.

4	small sweet potatoes	4
1/4 cup	vegetable oil	60 mL
1 tsp.	salt	5 mL
1/2 tsp.	freshly ground black pepper	2.5 mL

Preheat the oven to 375ºF (190ºC).

Peel the sweet potatoes and use a mandoline or sharp knife to cut them into slices 1/16-inch (.2-cm) thick.

Place the potato slices on a baking sheet lined with parchment paper or lightly oiled. Brush tops with oil and sprinkle with salt and pepper. Bake 12–15 minutes, until the edges curl and the slices are lightly browned. Transfer to a rack to cool. Repeat with the remaining potato slices if necessary.

The chips can be stored in an airtight container at room temperature for 1 week.

Crispy Potato Skins

Makes 4 servings

4 large	russet potatoes	4
1 Tbsp.	vegetable oil	15 mL
1/2 tsp.	garlic powder	2.5 mL
1 Tbsp.	freshly grated Parmesan cheese	15 mL

Crispy potato skins are an old-time favorite bar food, perfect for an informal gathering with friends.

Preheat the oven to 400°F (200°C).

Prick the potatoes with a fork in several places. Wrap in foil and bake until tender, about 50 minutes. Cool slightly before handling. The potatoes can be baked in advance and stored in the refrigerator for up to one day.

With a sharp knife, cut the potatoes into quarters. Scoop out the inside, leaving a 1/4-inch (.6-cm) shell. Reserve the filling for another use. Brush the skins with the oil. Place cut side up on a baking sheet. Bake about 15 minutes, or until crisp.

Remove from the oven. Sprinkle with the garlic powder and Parmesan cheese. Return to the oven for 2 minutes to melt the cheese. Transfer to a platter and serve immediately.

Herb-Stuffed Mushroom Caps

Makes 24 caps

For an exotic flavor, try using brown cremini mushrooms instead of white button mushrooms. Look for plump mushrooms with closed caps that are relatively the same size. They can be stuffed a day in advance, covered, refrigerated and baked as needed.

24	medium mushrooms, about 1 1/2 lbs. (680 g)	24
3 Tbsp.	butter	45 mL
1	small onion, finely chopped	1
1 tsp.	chopped fresh thyme, or 1/2 tsp. (2.5 mL) dried	5 mL
1/8 tsp.	paprika	.5 mL
1/2 tsp.	salt	2.5 mL
1/8 tsp.	freshly ground black pepper	.5 mL
1/2 cup	fresh bread crumbs	120 mL
1/4 cup	freshly grated Parmesan cheese	60 mL

Brush the mushrooms or wipe them clean with a damp cloth. Remove the stems and chop them finely. Set aside.

Melt the butter in a large non-stick frying pan over medium-high heat. Add the onion and cook for 5 minutes, or until soft. Add the mushroom stems, thyme, paprika, salt and pepper. Cook for 7 minutes, or until the mushrooms are soft. Remove from the heat. Stir in the bread crumbs and Parmesan cheese.

Preheat the oven to 375°F (190°C).

With a small spoon, stuff the mushroom centers with the filling. Arrange the mushroom caps in a single layer on a baking sheet. Bake 18–20 minutes, until the filling is hot and bubbly and the mushrooms are tender. Transfer to a platter and serve immediately.

Marinated Vegetables

Makes 6 servings

A marinated vegetable plate makes a crunchy, healthy appetizer. Don't marinate vegetables more than a few hours or they will lose their bright color.

1	small zucchini, cut into 1/4-inch (.6-cm) slices	1
1	red bell pepper, sliced into 1/4-inch (.6-cm) strips	1
1/2 cup	sliced mushrooms	120 mL
1/2 cup	broccoli florets	120 mL
1/2 cup	cauliflower florets	120 mL
2 Tbsp.	fresh lemon juice	30 mL
1 Tbsp.	red wine vinegar	15 mL
1 tsp.	sugar	5 mL
1 tsp.	Dijon mustard	5 mL
1 Tbsp.	fresh chopped oregano, or 1 tsp. (5 mL) dried	30 mL
1/2 cup	olive oil	120 mL
1 tsp.	salt	5 mL
1/2 tsp.	freshly ground black pepper	2.5 mL
1/4 cup	chopped fresh parsley	60 mL

Combine all the vegetables in a large bowl and set aside. Combine the lemon juice, red wine vinegar, sugar, mustard and oregano in a small bowl. Whisk in the olive oil. Pour the marinade over the vegetables and toss gently. Cover and refrigerate for up to 4 hours.

Remove the vegetables from the marinade. Season with salt and pepper. Arrange on a serving platter and sprinkle with the chopped parsley. Serve at room temperature.

Spicy Honey-Roasted Peanuts

Makes 3 cups (720 mL)

These nuts are positively addictive! Raw, unroasted peanuts are less salty and fresher tasting than roasted peanuts. They are available shelled in health food stores or in Asian food stores. You can also use unshelled peanuts and shell them yourself. Store unused, shelled nuts in the freezer up to 6 months for maximum flavor. A quick and easy presentation idea is to serve the nuts in a martini glass.

3 Tbsp.	butter	45 mL
3 Tbsp.	honey	45 mL
1 tsp.	Tabasco sauce	5 mL
1 tsp.	ground sea salt	5 mL
1 lb.	raw shelled peanuts	455 g

Preheat the oven to 300°F (150°C).

Melt the butter in a small saucepan over low heat. Stir in the honey, Tabasco and sea salt. Add the peanuts and stir well to coat.

Spread the nuts on a parchment-lined baking sheet. Bake for 25–30 minutes, stirring with a wooden spoon every 10 minutes to prevent the nuts from sticking together. Remove from the oven and let cool.

The nuts can be stored in an airtight container at room temperature for 2 weeks.

Spiced Pecans

Makes 2 cups (475 mL)

2 cups	pecans	475 mL
1	egg white, slightly beaten	1
1/2 cup	sugar	120 mL
1/2 tsp.	ground ginger	2.5 mL
1/4 tsp.	ground cinnamon	1.2 mL
1/4 tsp.	ground nutmeg	1.2 mL
1/2 tsp.	salt	2.5 mL

These spicy roasted pecans make the perfect hostess gift. Make a little extra for yourself and enjoy! Taking the time to roast the nuts first will bring out their sweet, natural flavor.

Roast the pecans in a dry, non-stick frying pan over low heat for 7 minutes. Be careful not to burn them. Remove from the heat and let cool.

Preheat the oven to 300°F (150°C).

Beat the egg whites, sugar, ginger, cinnamon, nutmeg and salt until frothy. Stir in the pecans and coat well. Spread the nuts on a parchment-lined baking sheet. Bake for 20 minutes, or until golden brown. Stir every 5 minutes to prevent them from sticking together. Remove from the heat and let cool.

The nuts can be stored in an airtight container at room temperature for 1 week.

Easy and
Elegant Entertaining

Occasionally you may want to impress your guests and offer appetizers that are extra special. This chapter is devoted to elegant foods that may call for ingredients that are slightly more expensive but readily available.

Appetizers such as Cucumber Rounds with Smoked Salmon Mousse, Marinated Mussels or Southwestern Crab Cakes with Ancho Tartar Sauce are perfect for a formal black-tie affair, an engagement party or entertaining a special business client. Rosemary Lamb Skewers, Grilled Garlic Shrimp or Scallop Seviche are spectacular served as a starter to a special dinner.

Marinated Lemon Olives

Makes 3/4 cup (180 mL)

1	lemon, washed and dried	1
2 tsp.	fennel seeds	10 mL
1/4 cup	extra-virgin olive oil	60 mL
1	clove garlic, minced	1
1 1/2 cups	black or green olives, rinsed and drained	360 mL

Using a zester or hand-held cheese grater, remove the peel, or zest, from the lemon. Chop it finely.

Toast the fennel seeds for 1 minute in a small frying pan over medium heat. Lower the heat and add the olive oil, garlic and lemon zest. Warm the mixture over low heat for 2 minutes. Do not let it get hot enough to burn the garlic or the mixture will taste bitter. Remove from the heat.

Place the olives in a glass bowl. Add the warm olive oil and toss well. Let stand at room temperature for several hours before serving to allow the flavors to blend.

Note: Olive oil becomes cloudy and thick when refrigerated, but returns to normal consistency at room temperature.

Zesty marinated lemon olives are great party finger food and make a perfect hostess gift. Place them in an attractive small jar and cover the olives with olive oil. Store in the refrigerator for up to 2 weeks. Use any Mediterranean variety of black or green olives, such as kalamata, Sicilian, and niçoise.

Zest

The zest is the colored outer layer of skin from citrus fruits. It is added to dishes for flavor, texture and color. A lemon zester is a handy tool that cuts a thread of rind when drawn across the fruit. You can then cut or chop the strips with a large knife. If you use a knife to remove the zest, be careful not to include any of the bitter white pith beneath the skin. A hand-held metal grater can also be used. Store citrus fruits with the rind removed in an airtight plastic bag to prevent them from drying out.

Marinated Lemon Shrimp

These marinated shrimp are a luxurious, sophisticated appetizer to serve at your next cocktail party. Guests will devour them quickly, so try to pass them on a platter rather than setting them on a table.

Makes 6—8 servings

5 cups	water	1.2 L
2 Tbsp.	white wine vinegar	30 mL
1	onion, chopped	1
1	bay leaf	1
1 lb.	shrimp in the shell	455 g
1/2 cup	olive oil	120 mL
1/4 cup	fresh lemon juice	60 mL
2 Tbsp.	white wine	30 mL
2 Tbsp.	chopped fresh basil	30 mL
1	clove garlic, minced	1
1/2 tsp.	salt	2.5 mL
1/4 tsp.	freshly ground black pepper	1.2 mL
	shredded lettuce	
	chopped fresh parsley	

Shrimp

When purchasing fresh shrimp, make sure they have not been previously frozen. Supermarkets sell individually quick-frozen shrimp in the freezer section, which enables you to use as many shrimp as the recipe requires. Extras can be kept frozen for later use. The size of the shrimp will determine cooking times. Black tiger shrimp from Thailand are my favorite and are usually sold bagged with 20 to 21 shrimps per lb. (455 g).

To de-vein shrimp is to remove the long black intestine that runs on the outside curve of the shrimp. This is not necessary if the shrimp are small in size. Using a small, sharp knife, slit the shrimp along the back and gently pull the vein. Rinse under cold water and pat dry.

Bring the water, vinegar, onion and bay leaf to a boil in a medium saucepan and simmer for 15 minutes. Add the shrimp and cook until they turn pink, about 3 minutes. Remove them with a slotted spoon and rinse immediately under cold water. Remove the shells and de-vein the shrimp.

In a large bowl, combine the olive oil, lemon juice, white wine, basil, garlic, salt and pepper. Add the shrimp and toss well to coat. Marinate for 30 minutes at room temperature. Serve on a platter lined with shredded lettuce and sprinkle with chopped parsley.

Grilled Garlic Shrimp

Makes 18 skewers

This luxurious and garlicky shrimp is wonderful served hot or at room temperature.

1/4 cup	dry white wine	60 mL
1 Tbsp.	fresh lemon juice	15 mL
3	cloves garlic, minced	3
1 Tbsp.	chopped fresh parsley	15 mL
1/2 tsp.	hot pepper flakes	2.5 mL
1 tsp.	salt	5 mL
1/4 cup	olive oil	60 mL
2 lbs.	large raw shrimp, peeled and de-veined, 20/21 count (see page 118)	900 g

Presoak 18 wooden skewers for 1 hour.

Combine the white wine, lemon juice, garlic, parsley, hot pepper flakes, salt and olive oil in a small bowl.

Thread 2 shrimps onto each presoaked skewer. Place the skewers in a shallow dish and pour the marinade over them. Cover and refrigerate for 30 minutes or up to 2 hours.

Heat the barbecue or broiler to high and brush the grill or broiler rack with oil. Remove the shrimp from the marinade and place on the grill. Brush with the marinade and grill 3 minutes on each side, until the shrimp are pink. Transfer to a platter and serve immediately.

Scallop Seviche

Makes 32 pieces

1/2 cup	fresh lime juice	120 mL
1/4 cup	tequila	60 mL
1/4 cup	chopped fresh cilantro	60 mL
2	cloves garlic, minced	2
1/4 cup	olive oil	60 mL
1 lb.	fresh scallops, shelled	455 g
	lettuce leaves	
	lime wedges	

Combine the lime juice, tequila, cilantro, garlic and olive oil in a large bowl. Add the scallops and toss well. Cover and refrigerate for 4 hours, or up to 1 day.

Remove the scallops from the marinade. Thread the scallops on wooden toothpicks, 2 per toothpick. Serve on a platter lined with lettuce leaves and garnish with lime wedges.

Seviche is a very popular method of preparing fish and seafood throughout Latin America. The fish is marinated in lemon or lime juice for several hours, a process that "cooks" the fish with the acid in the citrus juices. It is important to purchase the freshest, best-quality sea or bay scallops available.

Scallops

Bay scallops and sea scallops are available in your local fish department. Remove the tiny piece of tough tendon located where the scallop is attached to the shell.

Angels on Horseback

Bacon-wrapped oysters are showcased in this quick and classic party appetizer.

Makes 12 pieces

12	oysters, shucked	12
1 Tbsp.	fresh lemon juice	15 mL
2 Tbsp.	chopped fresh parsley	30 mL
	pinch cayenne pepper	
6	bacon slices, cut in half crosswise	6

Preheat the oven to 350°F (175°C).

In a small bowl, combine the oysters, lemon juice, parsley and cayenne. Cover and refrigerate for 30 minutes.

Place the bacon on a baking sheet and bake for 10 minutes, until partially cooked. Drain on paper towels.

Remove the oysters from the marinade and wrap 1 piece of bacon around each oyster, securing it with a wooden toothpick. Place the oysters seam side down on a baking sheet. Cook for 7 minutes, or until the bacon is crispy. Drain on paper towels. Serve hot.

Marinated Mussels

Makes approximately 12 pieces

1 lb.	mussels, about 24	455 g
3 Tbsp.	olive oil	45 mL
2 Tbsp.	fresh lemon juice	30 mL
2 Tbsp.	chopped fresh cilantro	30 mL
1 tsp.	Dijon mustard	5 mL
1	clove garlic, minced	1
	salt and freshly ground black pepper to taste	
1 cup	white wine	240 mL
2 cups	cold water	475 mL
1 Tbsp.	chopped red bell pepper (optional)	15 mL

This is a refreshing taste that is sure to please your guests. Mussels taste best when they are chilled. For an elegant presentation, serve them nestled on a platter lined with coarse, or pickling, salt, available in the spice section of your local supermarket.

Scrub the mussels and remove the beards. Discard any mussels with open or broken shells.

Combine the olive oil, lemon juice, cilantro, mustard, garlic, salt and pepper in a small bowl.

Bring the wine and water to a boil in a large saucepan. Add the mussels; reduce the heat and cover the pan. Cook 4 minutes, or until the mussels open. Remove the mussels with a slotted spoon, discarding any that are closed. Remove the mussels from their shells and place them in the marinade. Cover and marinate for 30 minutes in the refrigerator.

Select 12 shells for serving and discard the remaining shells. Arrange the mussel shells on crushed ice or coarse salt. Fill each shell with 2 mussels and some marinade. Sprinkle with red pepper if desired.

Southwestern Crab Cakes with Ancho Tartar Sauce

Makes 12 pieces

These tiny crab cakes get their spicy, smoky flavor from the chipotle chilies. Serve them with the Ancho Tartar Sauce or try a creamy Roasted Red Pepper Sauce (page 21).

1	egg, slightly beaten	1
1/4 cup	mayonnaise	60 mL
1 tsp.	dry mustard	5 mL
2 tsp.	finely chopped chipotle chili peppers	10 mL
1/4 cup	frozen corn, thawed	60 mL
2 Tbsp.	chopped green onions	30 mL
1	6-oz. (170-g) package frozen crabmeat, drained, cartilage removed (see page 33)	1
1/4 cup	dry bread crumbs	60 mL
1 Tbsp.	chopped fresh parsley	15 mL
1/2 tsp.	salt	2.5 mL
1/8 tsp.	freshly ground black pepper	.5 mL
1/2 cup	dry bread crumbs	120 mL
1 recipe	Ancho Tartar Sauce	1 recipe

Combine the egg, mayonnaise, dry mustard and chipotle peppers in a large bowl. Stir in the corn and green onions.

Squeeze out the excess liquid from the crab. Fold the crabmeat into the mayonnaise mixture. Add the 1/4 cup (60 mL) bread crumbs and parsley. Season with salt and pepper and mix well.

Shape the mixture into 12 small cakes, each about 1/4 inch (.6 cm) thick. If the mixture is too wet, add more bread crumbs. Place the remaining bread crumbs in a shallow dish. Coat the crab cakes with bread crumbs, shaking off the excess. Transfer to a platter, cover and chill for 30 minutes. This helps set the cakes and prevents them from falling apart when cooked.

Heat 1/4 inch (.6 cm) of vegetable oil in a large non-stick frying pan over medium-high heat. Add the crab cakes and cook 3 minutes on each side, or until brown. Drain on paper towels and serve hot with the tartar sauce.

Ancho Tartar Sauce

Makes 3/4 cup (180 mL)

A creamy mayonnaise-based sauce that goes well with spicy crab cakes, herb-breaded fish, or chicken strips. Ancho powder is smoked, dried poblano chili powder, and it's sold in most supermarkets. If it's unavailable, substitute cayenne pepper.

1/2 cup	mayonnaise	120 mL
1 Tbsp.	fresh lemon juice	15 mL
1 tsp.	Worcestershire sauce	5 mL
1/4 cup	chopped fresh cilantro	60 mL
1/2 tsp.	ancho powder	2.5 mL
1 tsp.	cayenne pepper	5 mL
	salt and freshly ground black pepper to taste	
1 Tbsp.	chopped fresh cilantro	15 mL

Combine the mayonnaise, lemon juice, Worcestershire sauce, cilantro, ancho powder and cayenne. Season with salt and pepper. Transfer to a serving bowl and sprinkle with the cilantro. Cover and refrigerate until ready to serve. The sauce can be stored in an airtight container in the refrigerator for 1 week.

Chipotle

Chipotle chilies are smoked jalapeños. They are available in a small can, preserved in adobo sauce—a vinegary tomato sauce. Extra chilies can be frozen and used later. Look for chipotle in adobo at your local supermarket.

Endive with Crabmeat

Makes 16–20 pieces

Belgian endive is also known as French endive and originates from the blanched roots of the chicory plant. Store endive in a plastic bag in the refrigerator and use it within 3 or 4 days. You can use the small leaves of romaine lettuce if endive is unavailable. This appetizer looks beautiful arranged on a silver platter with a single blossom placed in the center. You can substitute Chicken Almond Salad (page 139), Smoked Salmon Mousse (page 128), or Fresh Herb and Chèvre Spread (page 149) for the crab mixture.

1	4-oz. (113-g) package cream cheese, softened	1
1	6-oz. (170-g) can crabmeat, cartilage removed and drained	1
1 tsp.	fresh ginger, finely chopped	5 mL
2	heads Belgian endive	2
	watercress sprigs	

Combine the cream cheese, crabmeat and ginger in a small bowl. Cover and chill 30 minutes.

With a small sharp knife, trim off the bottom of each endive. Carefully remove the leaves. Rinse under cold water and pat dry.

To serve, arrange the leaves on a platter. Place a small teaspoon of filling on the bottom 1/3 of each endive leaf. Garnish with a watercress sprig.

Grilled Honey Dill Salmon Skewers

Makes 12 skewers

1¹/2 lbs.	salmon fillets, skin removed	680 g
¹/2 tsp.	salt	2.5 mL
¹/8 tsp.	freshly ground black pepper	.5 mL
1 Tbsp.	fresh lemon juice	15 mL
1 Tbsp.	Dijon mustard	15 mL
2 Tbsp.	honey	30 mL
1 tsp.	freshly chopped dill, or ¹/2 tsp. (2.5 mL) dried	5 mL
1	lemon, cut into wedges	1
1	sprig of fresh dill	1

Delicate strips of fresh salmon are brushed with a lemony dill glaze to produce an impressive, elegant appetizer. To prevent the salmon from sticking, clean the grill with a wire brush and oil it lightly.

Soak 12 wooden skewers in cold water for 1 hour.

Season the salmon fillets with salt and pepper. Cut the fish into ¹/4-inch (.6-cm) strips and thread them onto the soaked skewers. Be careful not to tear the salmon or pieces may fall from the skewers.

Combine the lemon juice, mustard, honey and chopped dill in a small bowl. Blend until smooth.

Heat the barbecue or broiler to high and brush the grill or broiler pan with oil. Cook the salmon for 2 minutes on each side, brushing with the glaze. The salmon should be cooked but still juicy. Use a thin knife to loosen the salmon pieces if they stick to the grill. Transfer to a serving platter and garnish with the lemon wedges and sprig of dill.

Cucumber Rounds With Smoked Salmon Mousse

Makes 24 pieces

For a spectacular presentation, pipe the mousse mixture onto the cucumber rounds and garnish with a sprig of watercress. To make it extra decorative, the cucumber can be scored with the tines of a fork or cut into shapes with cookie cutters. Place the cucumber rounds on a serving platter lined with a folded linen napkin.

1	8-oz. (225-g) package cream cheese, softened	1
3 oz.	smoked salmon	85 g
1 Tbsp.	fresh lemon juice	15 mL
2 tsp.	prepared horseradish	10 mL
1/4 tsp.	freshly ground black pepper	1.2 mL
3	English cucumbers	3
	watercress (optional)	

Combine the cream cheese, smoked salmon, lemon juice, horseradish and black pepper in a food processor or blender. Blend until the mixture is smooth. Cover and chill for 30 minutes before using.

Wash the cucumber and trim the ends. Slice each cucumber crosswise into 1-inch (2.5-cm) slices. With a melon-baller, scoop out the center of each slice, leaving a thin bottom layer for holding the filling. Transfer to a serving platter.

Spoon or pipe the mixture into the center of each cucumber round. Garnish each with a sprig of watercress, if desired. Cover and chill before serving.

Bacon-Wrapped Water Chestnuts

Makes 20 pieces

1/4 cup	soy sauce	60 mL
2 Tbsp.	rice vinegar	30 mL
1 Tbsp.	sugar	15 mL
1	8-oz. (227-mL) can whole water chestnuts, drained	1
10	uncooked bacon slices, cut in half crosswise	10

Combine the soy sauce, rice vinegar and sugar in a medium bowl. Add the water chestnuts and mix well. Cover and let stand at room temperature for 1 hour to blend the flavors.

Preheat the oven to 350°F (175°C).

Arrange the bacon slices in a single layer on a baking sheet. Bake for 10 minutes, until partially cooked. Drain on paper towels. Increase the oven temperature to 400°F (200°C).

Remove the water chestnuts from the marinade and wrap a piece of bacon around each one, securing the bacon with a wooden toothpick. Arrange on a baking sheet. Bake 15 minutes, until the bacon is crispy. Transfer to a platter and serve very hot.

This is an appetizer that requires a minimum of fuss, but provides maximum flavor. For an easy presentation idea, line a large platter with banana leaves and arrange the water chestnuts on the platter. To prevent the leaves from drying out and cracking, rub a small amount of vegetable oil onto the surface. Banana leaves are available fresh or frozen in Asian food stores and most supermarkets.

Soy Sauce

The most popular table condiment in China, soy sauce is made with fermented soybeans, wheat, salt and water. Look for a light soy sauce that has not been colored with the addition of molasses. Japanese soy sauce is lighter in flavor, has a more delicate taste and is preferred in dipping sauces. Soy sauce can be purchased in Asian stores and all supermarkets.

Prosciutto-Wrapped Asparagus

Makes 4 servings

Prosciutto is uncooked, air-dried, salt-cured ham from the regions of Parma and San Daniele in northern Italy. Purchase imported paper-thin slices of prosciutto—the domestic varieties are saltier and tougher. Mangos, figs and sliced melon are excellent substitutes for asparagus.

12	medium-size asparagus stalks	12
4 oz.	thinly sliced prosciutto	113 g

Peel the bottom $1/3$ of the asparagus with a vegetable peeler. Blanch the asparagus for 3 minutes in a large pot of boiling water. Remove with a slotted spoon and immerse in a bowl of ice water to cool. Drain and pat dry. The asparagus can be covered and stored in the refrigerator for up to 1 day.

Cut the prosciutto into 12 long strips lengthwise. Wrap 1 strip around the stem of each asparagus spear. Serve chilled or at room temperature.

Facing page: *Marinated Lemon Olives (p. 117)*.

Following page: *Marinated Mussels (p. 123)*.

Rosemary Lamb Skewers

Makes approximately 32 skewers

1¹/2 lbs.	lamb tenderloin	680 g
¹/2 cup	olive oil	120 mL
¹/4 cup	red wine vinegar	60 mL
3 Tbsp.	fresh lemon juice	45 mL
2	cloves garlic, minced	2
1 Tbsp.	chopped fresh rosemary	15 mL
4	medium red onions, sliced into 8 wedges	4
	salt and freshly ground black pepper to taste	
1 Tbsp.	lemon zest	15 mL

These Greek-inspired lamb skewers are redolent of rosemary and garlic. Substitute beef or pork cubes if you prefer. Prepare the skewers in advance, grill them just as guests are arriving and keep the skewers warm in the oven.

Trim the excess fat from the lamb. Cut it into 1-inch (2.5-cm) cubes. In a large bowl, combine the olive oil, red wine vinegar, lemon juice, garlic and rosemary. Add the cubed lamb and sliced onion. Toss well to coat. Cover and refrigerate for 6 hours or up to 24 hours.

Soak 32 wooden skewers for 1 hour in cold water.

Thread 2 pieces of lamb and 1 piece of onion onto each presoaked wooden skewer. Season with salt and pepper.

Heat the barbecue or broiler to high and brush the grill or broiler pan with oil. Cook the skewers for 3–4 minutes on each side, brushing with the marinade before grilling. Place on a platter and sprinkle with lemon zest. Serve hot.

Marinating

Marinating meat, poultry, fish and seafood prior to grilling adds flavor, and the high acid content of the marinade helps tenderize them. Do not marinate seafood or fish in an acid marinade for longer than 1 hour, or it will begin to "cook."

Parmesan Palmiers

Makes 36 pieces

Palmiers (palm leaves) are sweet, heart-shaped, puff pastry cookies dusted with sugar. This savory version calls for freshly grated Parmesan cheese and oregano. Serve them with a glass of chilled white wine for the perfect cocktail appetizer.

1/2 cup	freshly grated Parmesan cheese	120 mL
1 tsp.	chopped fresh oregano, or 1/2 tsp. (2.5 mL) dried	5 mL
1	1-lb. (455-g) package frozen puff pastry, thawed	1

Preheat the oven to 425°F (220°C). Line 2 baking sheets with parchment paper or plain brown paper.

Combine the Parmesan cheese and oregano in a small bowl. On a lightly floured surface, roll half the pastry out to a 14- by 10-inch (36- by 25-cm) rectangle. Sprinkle the pastry with half the cheese mixture. Lightly press the cheese into the dough.

Fold the two short sides, beginning with a 1-inch (2.5-cm) fold on each side, to almost meet in the center. Cut the pastry into $1/4$ inch (.6 cm) slices. Repeat with the remaining pastry. Place on the prepared baking sheet.

Bake for 10 minutes, or until golden brown. Transfer to a serving platter and serve immediately.

Cheddar Poppy Palmiers. Substitute $1/2$ cup (120 mL) finely grated white Cheddar cheese and 1 Tbsp. (15 mL) toasted poppy seeds for the Parmesan and oregano.

Parchment Paper

Using parchment paper to line baking sheets or cake pans prevents food from sticking and makes clean-up easy. It does not burn in the oven and the sheets can be reused several times. It's available at most supermarkets or houseware stores.

Jalapeño Cheddar Crackers

Makes 48 pieces

Easy and quick to prepare, these melt-in your-mouth crackers are perfect for a wine and cheese party. For a change, sprinkle finely chopped walnuts or pistachios on the crackers just before baking.

1/4 lb.	unsalted butter, chilled	113 g
1 cup	all-purpose flour	240 mL
1/2 lb.	sharp Cheddar cheese, grated	225 g
1/2 tsp.	freshly ground black pepper	2.5 mL
1 tsp.	salt	5 mL
1 tsp.	finely chopped jalapeño chili (see page 106)	5 mL

In a large mixing bowl, cream the butter and flour until smooth. Beat in the cheese, pepper, salt and jalapeño chili until well mixed.

Divide the dough into 2. Roll each piece into a log and wrap it in waxed paper. Chill for 3 hours or overnight.

Preheat the oven to 350°F (175°C).

With a thin knife, cut the logs into 1/4-inch (.6-cm) slices. Arrange on a baking sheet that's oiled or lined with parchment paper. Bake for 5 minutes until golden brown. Watch the crackers carefully as they burn easily. Transfer to a rack and let cool.

The crackers can be made up to 6 hours in advance and stored in an airtight container at room temperature. They keep in the freezer for 1 month.

Corn Muffins with Smoked Honey Ham

Makes 24 pieces

1 cup	all-purpose flour	240 mL
1 cup	yellow cornmeal	240 mL
2 Tbsp.	sugar	30 mL
1/2 tsp.	salt	2.5 mL
1 Tbsp.	baking powder	15 mL
1 cup	milk	240 mL
1	egg	1
2 Tbsp.	vegetable oil	30 mL
1/4 cup	melted butter	60 mL
1/2 cup	frozen corn, chopped	120 mL
1/4 cup	mango chutney	60 mL
4 oz.	smoked honey ham, thinly sliced	113 g

These irresistible bite-size muffins are spread with mango chutney and filled with thinly sliced, smoked honey ham. Smoked turkey or chicken can be substituted for the ham. A pretty presentation is to arrange the muffins on a flat wicker or rattan basket, lined with a checked cloth napkin.

Preheat the oven to 400ºF (200ºC).

Combine the flour, cornmeal, sugar, salt and baking powder in a large bowl. Combine the milk, egg, oil and melted butter in a medium bowl. Mix well. Add the milk mixture to the flour mixture and stir just until moistened. Stir in the corn.

Spoon the batter into a greased mini muffin pan. Bake for 15 minutes, or until golden brown. Cool on a rack for 5 minutes. Remove from the pan. When completely cool, the muffins can be stored in an airtight container at room temperature for up to 3 days.

To serve, slice the muffins in half. Spread the bottoms with the mango chutney, top with sliced smoked honey ham and replace the muffin top.

Thai Shrimp Toasts

These crispy, golden
appetizers are easy to
prepare and can be
reheated as guests
arrive.

Makes 32 pieces

24	medium shrimp, peeled and deveined	24
1	egg	1
2	green onions, chopped	2
2 Tbsp.	chopped fresh cilantro	30 mL
1 Tbsp.	fish sauce	15 mL
1 tsp.	grated fresh ginger	5 mL
1 tsp.	freshly ground black pepper	5 mL
8	slices white bread	8
1 recipe	Lime Dipping Sauce (page 66)	1 recipe

Grind the shrimp finely in a food processor. Add the egg,
green onions, cilantro, fish sauce, ginger and pepper. Pulse
for 3 seconds. Scrape down the bowl with a spatula. Pulse for
3 more seconds. Set aside.

Remove the crusts from the bread and slice each piece into
4 triangles. Spread a spoonful of filling evenly on each piece.

Heat 1 inch (2.5 cm) of oil in a wok or deep pot to 375°F
(190°C). Fry the shrimp triangles a few at a time, topping side
down, for 2 minutes. Flip them over and fry for 2 minutes
longer or until golden brown. Drain on paper towels. Transfer
to a warm serving platter. Serve with the dipping sauce.

The triangles can be fried ahead of time and reheated in a
400°F (200°C) oven for 10 minutes.

Fish Sauce

A basic flavoring in Thai and Vietnamese cooking, fish sauce (*nam pla* in
Thai; **nouc mam** in Vietnamese) is the pale brown liquid collected from fish
that has been salted and fermented in jars. It has a strong fishy smell that
disappears when cooked. Purchase a brand from Thailand — Squid or
Golden Boy are both excellent brands.

Sausage Rolls

Makes 80 pieces

| 1 | 1-lb. (455-g) frozen package puff pastry, thawed | 1 |
| 1 lb. | sausage meat | 455 g |

Try to use a high-quality, well-seasoned beef or pork sausage from your local butcher for these light pastry puffs.

On a lightly floured surface roll the puff pastry into a rectangle ⅛ inch (.3 cm) thick. Cut it into 3 strips, each 3 inches (7.5 cm) wide. Place the meat along the center of each piece. Roll up each strip lengthwise, jelly-roll fashion, making sure the dough overlaps. Wet the edge of the dough with water and press it firmly to secure. Cover and chill for 1 hour. The sausage rolls can be made to this point and stored in an airtight container in the freezer for 1 month.

Preheat the oven to 400°F (200°C).

Cut the sausage logs into 1-inch (2.5-cm) slices. Arrange on a baking sheet lined with parchment paper. Bake for 15 minutes, or until puffed and golden. Serve hot.

Pâté à Choux with Chicken Almond Salad

Makes approximately 20

Pâté à choux is the French name for these rich tiny popovers, which are filled with sweet cream or savory fillings. Gruyère cheese can be mixed into the dough to make gougères, a specialty of the Burgundy region of France. To achieve uniformly sized puffs, use a pastry bag and pipe the dough onto a parchment-lined baking sheet. I like to arrange the popovers on a silver platter sprinkled with a few rose petals for a colorful presentation.

1/2 cup	water	120 mL
1/4 cup	butter	60 mL
1/2 tsp.	salt	2.5 mL
1/2 cup	all-purpose flour	120 mL
2	eggs	2
1 recipe	Chicken Almond Salad	1 recipe

Bring the water and butter to a boil in a medium saucepan. Remove from the heat. Add the salt and flour. Return to the heat and beat vigorously until the mixture forms a smooth ball. Remove from the heat. Beat in the eggs, one at a time, until the mixture is smooth.

Preheat the oven to 400°F (200°C).

Drop the batter by spoonfuls, 1 inch (2.5 cm) apart, onto a baking sheet lined with parchment paper. Dip your finger in warm water or egg wash and shape the rounds, smoothing the tops.

Bake for 15 minutes. Reduce the heat to 350°F (175°C) and cook 8 minutes longer, until the puffs are no longer sticky in the center. Cool on a rack. The pastry can be stored in an airtight container at room temperature for 2 days or frozen for 1 month. Thaw at room temperature prior to using.

Slice the puffs in half horizontally. Pipe or spoon the Chicken Almond Salad onto the bottom half of each puff. Replace the tops. Place on a baking sheet and bake in a preheated 350°F (175°C) oven for 12 minutes, until the filling is warm.

Chicken Almond Salad

Makes 1 cup (240 mL)

This crunchy mixture can be spooned into baked tart shells, crèpes or pastry puffs.

1/2 cup	cooked chicken breast, shredded	120 mL
1/4 cup	finely chopped almonds	60 mL
1/4 cup	light mayonnaise	60 mL
1 tsp.	Dijon mustard	5 mL
1/2 tsp.	fresh lemon juice	2.5 mL
1 Tbsp.	chopped fresh dill	15 mL
1/4 tsp.	salt	1.2 mL
1/8 tsp.	freshly ground black pepper	.5 mL

In a large bowl, combine the chicken and almonds. Stir in the mayonnaise, Dijon mustard, lemon juice and dill. Season with salt and pepper. Cover and refrigerate until serving time.

The mixture can be stored in an airtight container in the refrigerator for 3 days.

Cranberry-Apple Chicken Tartlets

Makes 24 tartlets

Dried cranberries add a tart note to these sweet crunchy appetizers. They are available in most supermarkets. Soak dried cranberries in hot water for 10 minutes to make them plump, juicy and tender.

1/2 tsp.	salt	2.5 mL
1	bay leaf	1
1	small onion, chopped	1
6	black peppercorns	6
1 lb.	boneless, skinless chicken breasts	455 g
1/4 cup	mayonnaise	60 mL
1/4 cup	apricot preserves	60 mL
2 tsp.	lemon juice	10 mL
2	green onions, finely chopped	2
	pinch ground cinnamon	
1/4 cup	dried cranberries	60 mL
1	large Granny Smith apple, peeled and finely chopped	1
1/2 tsp.	salt	1.2 mL
1/8 tsp.	pepper	.5 mL
24	baked Tartlet Shells (page 158)	24
2 Tbsp.	chopped pecans (optional)	30 mL

Combine the salt, bay leaf, onion and peppercorns in a large pot of water and bring to a boil. Add the chicken. Reduce the heat and cook for 12–15 minutes, or until the chicken is no longer pink. Remove the chicken and let cool.

With a sharp knife, cut the chicken into 1/4-inch (.6-cm) cubes. Combine the mayonnaise, apricot preserves, lemon juice, green onions and cinnamon in a large bowl. Add the chicken, cranberries and apple. Toss well to coat. Season with salt and pepper. Spoon into the prebaked tartlet shells and garnish with chopped pecans, if desired.

Mini Quiche Lorraine

Makes 40–48 pieces

40–48	unbaked Tartlet Shells (page 158)	40–48
3	eggs	3
1 cup	heavy cream	240 mL
1/4 cup	milk	60 mL
1/4 tsp.	dry mustard	1.2 mL
1/8 tsp.	cayenne	.5 mL
1/2 tsp.	salt	2.5 mL
1/4 tsp.	freshly ground black pepper	1.2 mL
8	slices bacon, cooked and crumbled	8
1 cup	grated Swiss cheese	240 mL
2 Tbsp.	chopped fresh chives (optional)	30 mL

Quiche originated in the Lorraine area of France and usually contains eggs, butter, bacon and heavy cream. This version adds Swiss cheese and chopped green onions. Store-bought tart shells can be used to cut the preparation time in half.

Preheat the oven to 350ºF (175ºC).

Beat the eggs, cream and milk together in a large bowl. Add the mustard, cayenne, salt and pepper. Blend well.

Divide the bacon and cheese evenly among the tart shells. Pour the egg mixture into the shells. Bake for 10–12 minutes, until the centers are set and the tops are golden brown. Remove from the oven and cool slightly. Sprinkle with chives if desired.

The tarts can be made in advance, refrigerated, and reheated in a 250ºF (120ºC) oven for 7 minutes.

⚘ Tortilla Pesto Pizza

Makes 32 pieces

Flour tortillas make a
quick and easy
pizza—perfect for
unannounced guests or
hungry children. Use
store-bought pesto if
you haven't any
homemade on hand.

4	8-inch (20-cm) flour tortillas	4
2 Tbsp.	olive oil	30 mL
3/4 cup	Pesto (page 168)	180 mL
1/2 cup	freshly grated mozzarella cheese	120 mL

Preheat the oven to 375°F (190°C).

Brush the tortillas with olive oil. Place them on a baking sheet and bake for 4 minutes until crisp. Remove from the oven.

Spread each tortilla with pesto. Sprinkle with the grated cheese. Return to the oven and bake for 7 minutes, until the cheese melts. Cut the tortillas into 8 wedges and serve immediately.

Roast Beef and Chive Butter Canapés

Makes 36 pieces

18	mini bagels	18
1/2 cup	butter softened	120 mL
3 Tbsp.	chopped fresh chives	45 mL
2 Tbsp.	Dijon mustard	30 mL
1 tsp.	prepared horseradish	5 mL
1/2 lb.	cooked roast beef, thinly sliced	225 g
36	capers, drained and rinsed	36

Small cocktail-size bagels are perfect topped with thin slices of rare roast beef and a creamy chive butter. Increase the horseradish if you like to give it a pungent bite.

Preheat the oven to 375°F (190°C).

Cut the bagels in half with a knife and arrange them on a baking sheet. Bake for 5 minutes, or until lightly toasted. Remove from the oven and let cool.

In a small bowl, combine the butter, chives, Dijon mustard and horseradish. Beat the mixture until it's smooth and fluffy.

Cut the roast beef into 1-inch (2.5-cm) strips. Spread the chive butter on the cut side of the toasted bagels. Top with the roast beef and garnish with a caper.

Tuna and Potato Croquettes

Makes 12 pieces

This recipe is inspired by the classic Italian combination of tuna and potatoes. Croquettes are tiny fritters and are popular throughout Italy. They are best served at room temperature. To eliminate frying the croquettes, place them on a lightly greased baking sheet and bake in a preheated 350°F (175°C) oven for 15–20 minutes, or until crispy.

2	medium potatoes	2
2 Tbsp.	milk	30 mL
1	6-oz. (170-g) can tuna packed in oil, drained	1
1	egg	1
2 Tbsp.	green onion, finely chopped	30 mL
1 Tbsp.	fresh lemon juice	15 mL
	salt and freshly ground black pepper to taste	
1	egg, lightly beaten	1
1/4 cup	fine bread crumbs	60 mL

Place the potatoes in a pot of cold water and bring to a boil. Reduce the heat and simmer 10 minutes, or until the potatoes are tender when pierced with a fork. Drain and cool slightly.

Mash the potato with the milk. Measure out 1 cup (240 mL) and combine it with the tuna, egg, onion and lemon juice. Season with salt and pepper. Cover and refrigerate for 1 hour or until the mixture is firm enough to roll.

Shape the potato mixture into small 1-inch (2.5-cm) logs. Roll each log in beaten egg, then the bread crumbs. Shake off excess crumbs just before frying.

Heat 1 inch (2.5-cm) of vegetable oil in a wok or deep pot to 375°F (190°C). Fry the croquettes until golden brown, about 2 minutes per side. Drain on paper towels. The croquettes can be fried ahead of time, refrigerated for up to 6 hours and reheated at 400°F (200°C) for 8 minutes.

Potato Latkes

Makes 20 pieces

2	eggs, slightly beaten	2
1 tsp.	salt	5 mL
1/2 tsp.	freshly ground black pepper	2.5 mL
1/4 cup	finely chopped green onions	60 mL
4	medium potatoes, about 1 1/2 lbs. (680 g)	4
2 Tbsp.	all-purpose flour	30 mL
1/2 tsp.	baking powder	2.5 mL
	sour cream or Crème Fraîche (page 167)	
2 Tbsp.	chopped fresh chives	30 mL

Latkes—potato pancakes—are traditionally served at Hanukkah. I like to make them small and serve them as bite-size appetizers. To vary them, top with smoked salmon or caviar.

Beat the eggs with salt and pepper until frothy. Add the green onions. Peel and finely grate the potatoes and add them to the egg mixture (this will prevent the potatoes from discoloring). Blend in the flour and baking powder. Mix well.

Heat 1/2 inch (1.2 cm) oil in a large frying pan over medium-high heat. Drop the batter by spoonfuls into the hot oil and flatten with a spoon. Cook about 2 minutes on each side until they are crisp and golden. Drain on paper towels. Add more oil to the pan if necessary. Repeat with the remaining batter. Serve hot, topped with sour cream or crème fraîche and chives.

The latkes can be made ahead and reheated in a 400°F (200°C) oven until hot, about 10 minutes.

Baby Red Potatoes with Sour Cream and Caviar

Makes 24 pieces

An easy, sophisticated appetizer that can be topped with a selection of caviar. Sturgeon roe is the highest quality caviar and comes in several varieties — beluga, osetra and sevruga (gray to black in color). Depending on your budget, you can use roe from salmon, which is bright red, or Canadian whitefish, a golden color. If caviar is not to your taste or budget, substitute chopped nuts, crumbled bacon or grated Cheddar cheese.

12	small red potatoes	12
1 tsp.	salt	5 mL
1/4 cup	sour cream	60 mL
1 oz.	caviar	28 g
24	dill sprigs	24

Gently scrub the potatoes. Do not peel them. Place them in a large saucepan, cover with cold water, add the salt and bring to a boil. Cook about 10 minutes, until the potatoes are tender. Drain well and cool completely. The potatoes can be stored in a covered container in the refrigerator for 1 day. Bring them back to room temperature before proceeding.

Cut the potatoes in half and place them cut side down on a platter. Using a melon-baller, scoop out a small amount of the uncut side of each potato half. Fill with a dollop of sour cream and top with caviar. Garnish each with a small sprig of dill.

Facing page: *Corn Muffins with Smoked Honey Ham (p. 135).*

Polenta Squares with Roasted Red Pepper Sauce

Makes 32 pieces

7 cups	water	1.7 L
1 tsp.	salt	5 mL
1 3/4 cups	fine yellow cornmeal	420 mL
2 Tbsp.	olive oil	30 mL
3/4 cup	Roasted Red Pepper Sauce (page 21)	180 mL

Bring the water and salt to a boil in a heavy pot. Add the cornmeal in a thin stream, whisking constantly to prevent the cornmeal from lumping. Cook for 30 minutes over low heat, stirring constantly with a wooden spoon. Pour the mixture onto a baking sheet to cool. The polenta should be about 1/2 inch (1.2 cm) thick.

When the polenta is cool, cut it into squares with a sharp knife.

Heat the oil to medium-high in a large non-stick frying pan. Add the polenta in a single layer and fry for 2 minutes, or until crisp and golden on one side. Place on a serving platter. Serve warm or at room temperature with Roasted Red Pepper Sauce.

The polenta squares can be stored in an airtight container in the refrigerator for 2 days before frying.

Polenta is yellow cornmeal cooked into a thick porridge. It can be eaten hot, with butter and cheese, or the mixture can be cooled on a baking sheet, cut into squares and then grilled, baked or fried. Serve with a dollop of red pepper sauce or creamy Pesto Dip (page 19). When cooking polenta, stir it constantly with a wooden spoon and watch carefully so it doesn't burn.

Facing page: *Tortilla Pesto Pizza (p. 142).*

Cherry Tomatoes with Fresh Herb and Chèvre Spread

Makes 40 pieces

A variety of creamy fillings can be used to fill these bite-size morsels. Look for bright red cherry tomatoes that have a sweet flavor.

40	large firm cherry tomatoes	40
1 cup	Fresh Herb and Chèvre Spread	240 mL
40	parsley sprigs	40
	lettuce leaves	

With a small, sharp knife, cut off the stem top of each cherry tomato. Remove the seeds and pulp with a melon-baller or a small spoon. Place the tomatoes, cut side down, on a baking sheet lined with paper towels. Let drain in the refrigerator until ready to use. The tomatoes can be prepared up to 8 hours in advance.

Place the herb spread in a pastry bag or use a small spoon. Pipe or spoon the mixture into the tomatoes and garnish each with a sprig of parsley. Place on a serving platter lined with lettuce leaves to prevent the tomatoes from rolling around. Cover and chill until ready to serve.

Goat Cheese

Goat cheese, or chèvre in French, has a sharp, tangy flavor. Purchase a young, fresh goat cheese with no rind, which has a mild flavor and creamy texture. Older goat cheese is much stronger in flavor and has a dry, mealy texture. Store the cheese in the refrigerator wrapped in plastic for up to 4 days.

Fresh Herb and Chèvre Spread

Makes 1 cup (240 mL)

French Boursin or Rondele-style herbed cream cheese is available in supermarkets or gourmet food shops. You can also use this tangy, creamy spread as a dip with raw vegetables, or spread it on crackers.

4 oz.	chèvre cheese	113 g
4 oz.	herbed cream cheese, Boursin or Rondele	113 g
1 Tbsp.	chopped fresh parsley	15 mL
1 Tbsp.	fresh thyme, or 1 tsp. (5 mL) dried	15 mL
1 Tbsp.	olive oil	15 mL
1/8 tsp.	freshly ground black pepper	.5 mL

Combine all the ingredients, mixing well. The spread can be stored in an airtight container in the refrigerator for 5 days and brought back to room temperature before serving.

Vegetable Tempura with Dipping Sauce

Makes 8 servings

These delicate, tender, deep-fried vegetables are a favorite Japanese snack food. The secret to successful tempura is to ensure that the batter is cold and the oil temperature remains at 375°F (190°C). Make sure the pieces to be deep-fried are the same size. If the oil is not hot enough, the food will absorb too much oil and will be greasy. Use a deep-fat thermometer or try this simple test: drop a cube of white bread into the oil; if it browns in 60 seconds, the oil is hot enough.

1	egg, slightly beaten	1
1 cup	ice-cold water	240 mL
1 cup	flour	240 mL
1/2 tsp.	baking soda	2.5 mL
1/2 tsp.	salt	2.5 mL
1/4 cup	each thinly sliced zucchini, onions, broccoli, mushrooms and eggplant	60 mL
1 recipe	Dipping Sauce	1 recipe

In a large bowl, beat the egg with the ice water. Gradually add the flour, baking soda and salt. Do not overmix or you will have a heavy batter.

Heat 1 inch (2.5 cm) of vegetable oil in a wok or large frying pan until it reaches 375°F (190°C) on a deep-fat thermometer. Working with a few at a time, dip the vegetables into the batter and gently lower them into the hot oil. Cook for 1 minute on each side until golden. Do not overcrowd the pan. Remove with a slotted spoon and drain on paper towels. Repeat with the remaining vegetables. Serve immediately with the dipping sauce.

Daikon

Daikon radish is also known as Oriental radish or Japanese radish and comes from the same family as the familiar red round radish. Daikon is a large vegetable, 1 to 2 pounds (455 to 900 g), and is available year-round in the specialty produce section of supermarkets. Choose a firm, smooth radish with a white creamy interior. Store in the refrigerator for up to 3 days; if stored too long, radishes lose their moisture and become flavorless. Daikon can be served raw in salads, as a crudité or pickled in a garlicky brine. Oriental cooks use daikon in stir-fry and it makes a tasty addition to soups and stews.

Dipping Sauce

Makes 2 cups (475 mL)

This classic dipping sauce is always served with crispy tempura. Purchase a Japanese soy sauce, which has a clean light flavor. (Chinese soy sauce usually contains molasses added during the brewing process, which makes the flavor too strong.) Konbu is sun-dried sea kelp and is available in Japanese food shops.

1/2 oz.	konbu	14 g
2 cups	water	475 mL
1/3 cup	mirin, or rice wine	80 mL
1/3 cup	soy sauce	80 mL
1/2 cup	grated daikon radish	120 mL
1 tsp.	grated fresh ginger	5 mL

Place the konbu and water in a saucepan and bring to a boil. Lower the heat, cover and simmer for 20 minutes. Strain the liquid and discard the konbu.

In a small saucepan, combine the konbu stock, mirin and soy sauce. Bring to a boil and lower the heat. Keep warm until serving time. Serve in small bowls with some daikon and ginger in each bowl.

The sauce can be made 6 hours in advance, stored in an airtight container in the refrigerator and warmed before serving.

Mirin

Mirin is a Japanese sweet rice wine that can be used in salad dressings or marinades. It is available in Asian markets. Dry sherry can be substituted for mirin.

Brie en Croute

Makes 6 servings

En croute means to encase food with pastry and bake until golden brown and puffy. You can substitute any of the many soft-ripened cheeses, such as French Camembert, Vacherin Mont d'Or or Chaource, for Brie. Serve with crusty French bread, tart green apple wedges, Anjou pear slices and a glass of California Merlot. Freeze the other 1/2 of the puff pastry to use later.

1/2	1-lb. (455-g) package frozen puff pastry, thawed	1/2
1	6-oz. (170-g) wheel of Brie cheese	1
1	egg, beaten	1

Roll out the puff pastry on a lightly floured surface. Place the cheese in the center of the pastry and gather up the edges to enclose the cheese. Be careful not to tear the pastry or the cheese will run out when cooked. Pinch the top together. A small bundle of dough will form on top; trim the excess with scissors. Place on a parchment-lined baking sheet. The parchment paper will help prevent the cheese from sticking to the pan and it will slide off easily. Cover and chill for 1 hour.

Preheat the oven to 400°F (200°C). Brush the egg wash on the pastry. Bake for 20–25 minutes, until the pastry is golden brown. Gently slide the Brie from the baking sheet to a platter. Serve warm.

Choosing Ripe Brie or Camembert

Ripe cheese will have a yellowish rind. The cut cheese will ooze slightly when pressed and have a fruity aroma and creamy yellow interior color. An under-ripe Brie or Camembert will be firm to the touch and have a chalky core; over-ripe cheese will be runny, with a brownish rind and smell of ammonia.

Baked Camembert with Sun-Dried Tomato Pesto

Makes 4 servings

1	8-oz. (225-g) round Camembert cheese	1
8	dry-packed sun-dried tomatoes	8
1	clove garlic, minced	1
2 Tbsp.	chopped fresh parsley	30 mL
3 Tbsp.	pine nuts, toasted	45 mL
1 Tbsp.	olive oil	15 mL

This is a quick and easy way to serve a wheel of cheese. A delicious quick dinner can be made by thinning this tomato pesto with water and tossing it with hot pasta.

Place the cheese in an ovenproof serving dish. Place the sundried tomatoes in a small bowl. Cover with hot water and let sit for 15 minutes, until the tomatoes are soft. Discard the liquid.

Preheat the oven to 400°F (200°C).

Combine the garlic, parsley, pine nuts and sun-dried tomatoes in a food processor or blender. Process until the mixture is chunky. With the motor running, add the oil slowly. Spread the mixture over the Camembert. Bake the cheese for 10 minutes, or until it begins to melt. Serve warm, with crackers or toasted French bread.

Basic Recipes

In this chapter, you will find a collection of recipes that are used to produce dishes throughout the book. They can all be made ahead, and once you have mastered these basic recipes, you can quickly produce an array of appetizers or dishes to serve for lunch or dinner. To save time, store-bought versions of these recipes are readily available and can be substituted for homemade.

Basic Pastry Dough

Makes 2 pie shells or 36 tartlets

This dough is perfect for tartlet shells or pies.

2 1/2 cups	all-purpose flour	600 mL
1 tsp.	salt	5 mL
1/2 lb.	vegetable shortening or lard	225 g
1/2 cup	cold milk	120 mL
1	egg, lightly beaten	1

Combine the flour and salt in the bowl of the food processor. Cut the shortening or lard into small pieces and add it to the flour. Process briefly until the mixture resembles coarse meal.

Add the milk a little at a time and then the beaten egg. Divide the dough in half. Form into 2 balls and cover with plastic wrap. Chill in the refrigerator for 30 minutes before using, or up to 2 days. The dough can be frozen for up to 2 months.

Tartlet Shells

These tartlet shells are easy to make and can be prepared days in advance.

Makes 36 small tartlet shells

| 1 recipe | Basic Pastry Dough (page 157) | 1 recipe |

On a lightly floured surface, roll the dough into ⅛-inch (.3-cm) thickness. With a 3-inch (7.5-cm) cookie cutter, cut out as many rounds as possible. Place the pastry rounds into tart shells or mini muffin tins. Press firmly and cut off the excess pastry with a knife.

Line each pastry shell with foil and fill with pie weights or dried beans. Bake in a preheated 400°F (200°C) oven for 15 minutes or until golden brown. Remove the weights and foil. Cool slightly. Gently remove from the tart shell or muffin tin.

The tartlet shells can be stacked between waxed paper in an airtight container at room temperature for 3 days.

Bouchées

Makes 36 pieces

1	1-lb. (455-g) package frozen puff pastry, thawed	1
1	egg, beaten	1

Preheat the oven to 400ºF (200ºC).

On a lightly floured surface, roll the pastry dough to ⅛-inch (.3-cm) thickness. With a small cookie cutter, cut out as many circles as the pastry allows.

With a smaller cookie cutter, cut out and remove the centers of half the pastry rounds. Set the centers aside. Brush the whole rounds with the beaten egg. Place the pastry rings over top. Press firmly.

With a knife, score the tops in a lattice pattern. Arrange on a baking sheet lined with parchment paper. Bake for 8 minutes, or until puffy and golden brown. Remove from the heat and let cool. Remove any dough that has risen in the center of the rounds.

The bouchées can be stored in an airtight container at room temperature for 2 days.

A bouchée (little mouthful) is a small puff pastry round filled with a sweet or savory filling. I like to fill them with delicate pieces of crab or spicy curried chicken. The leftover centers can be frozen and baked later as simple crackers or croutons sprinkled with grated cheese.

Bread Cups

These tiny toasted bread cups are perfect for holding a variety of fillings.

Makes 48

3 Tbsp.	butter, melted	45 mL
12	slices white bread	12

Preheat the oven to 350°F (175°C).

Brush 2 mini muffin pans with the melted butter. Flatten the bread with a rolling pin. Trim off the crusts and cut each slice into 4 squares. Press the squares into the prepared pans. Bake 10 minutes, or until golden. Remove from the oven and let cool in the pans.

The bread cups can be stored in an airtight container at room temperature for 3 days or frozen for 1 month.

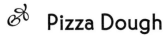

Pizza Dough

Makes 2 small pizzas

Pizza dough can be refrigerated for up to a day or frozen for a month.

1 tsp.	sugar	5 mL
3/4 cup	warm water, no hotter than 105⁰F (40°C)	180 mL
1	envelope active dry yeast, or 1 Tbsp. (15 mL)	1
2 1/2 cups	all-purpose flour	600 mL
1 tsp.	salt	5 mL
2 Tbsp.	olive oil	30 mL

Dissolve the sugar in the warm water. Sprinkle the yeast over the water and let rest for 5 minutes, or until the mixture starts to bubble. If the yeast does not bubble, throw it away and start again.

Combine the flour and salt. Mix the olive oil and the yeast mixture in a large bowl. Add the flour mixture to the yeast mixture, stirring with a wooden spoon.

Turn the dough out onto a lightly floured surface and knead for about 15 minutes, adding a little more flour if the dough sticks to your hands. Place the dough in an oiled bowl. Turn the dough until it's coated on all sides with oil. Cover the bowl with plastic wrap and place in a warm place to rise until doubled in size, about 1 hour. Punch down before using in a recipe or freezing.

❧ Crostini

Makes approximately 24 pieces

1	baguette	1
1/2 cup	extra-virgin olive oil	120 mL

Crostini are small pieces of toasted country bread on which the Northern Italians spread a variety of toppings, chicken liver being the most popular. The bread should be a day old and have a good thick crust. Crostini can be used in salads, with dips or spreads or crushed into soup.

Preheat the oven to 350ºF (175ºC).

Cut the bread into 1/2-inch (1.2-cm) slices. Brush each slice with olive oil.

Arrange the slices on a baking sheet. Bake for about 10 minutes, or until lightly brown. Cool on a rack.

Crostini can be stored in an airtight container at room temperature for 2 weeks.

Sesame Wonton Crackers

Makes 24

These are a quick alternative to using store-bought crackers for dips or spreads.

2 Tbsp.	soy sauce	30 mL
1 tsp.	sesame oil	5 mL
24	3-inch (7.5-cm) square wonton wrappers	24
2 Tbsp.	toasted sesame seeds	30 mL

Preheat the oven to 400°F (200°C).

Combine the soy sauce and sesame oil in a small bowl. Arrange the wonton wrappers on a parchment-lined baking sheet. Brush them with the soy sauce mixture and sprinkle them evenly with sesame seeds. Bake for 5 minutes, until golden brown. Transfer to a rack and let cool. The chips can be stored in an airtight container at room temperature for 1 week.

Sesame Oil

Sesame oil is made from toasted, crushed sesame seeds. It is used for seasoning, not for frying. The quality of the oil varies greatly. Look for a Japanese brand if possible—Kadoya is a good choice and is available in Chinese markets and some supermarkets. Store opened sesame oil in the refrigerator.

❧ Pumpernickel Toast Points

Makes 24

Small loaves of cocktail pumpernickel bread can be found in the deli section of most supermarkets. Rye bread can also be used in this recipe.

| 24 | thin slices cocktail-type pumpernickel bread | 24 |
| 2 Tbsp. | extra-virgin olive oil | 30 mL |

Preheat the oven to 350ºF (175ºC).

Cut each pumpernickel slice on the diagonal. Brush with the oil. Arrange the slices on a baking sheet and bake until crisp, about 10–12 minutes. Transfer to a rack and let cool.

The toast points can be stored in an airtight container at room temperature for 2 weeks.

Rainbow Tortilla Chips

Makes 48 chips

2	8-inch (20-cm) flour tortillas	2
2	8-inch (20-cm) yellow corn tortillas	2
2	8-inch (20-cm) blue corn tortillas	2
1/4 cup	vegetable oil	60 mL
1 tsp.	chili powder	5 mL

When making these chips, try to use a combination of white (wheat flour), yellow (corn flour) and blue (blue corn flour) for a colorful assortment. You can find blue tortillas at gourmet food shops.

Preheat the oven to 350°F (175°C).

Lay the tortillas on a cutting board. Brush them lightly with oil and sprinkle with chili powder. Cut each tortilla into 8 wedges.

Arrange the wedges in a single layer on a non-stick baking sheet. Bake until lightly browned, about 9 minutes. Watch them carefully as they burn easily. Transfer to a rack and let cool.

The chips can be stored in an airtight container at room temperature for up to 2 weeks.

Pita Chips

Makes 36 wedges

A low-fat alternative to serving potato chips with dips and spreads. Perfect for dipping or just munching as chips.

1 Tbsp.	sesame seeds	15 mL
6	small whole wheat pita breads	6
1	egg white, slightly beaten	1

Preheat the oven to 350ºF (175ºC).

Toast the sesame seeds for 1 minute over low heat in a small frying pan. Remove from the heat.

Brush the pita with the egg white. Sprinkle with the toasted sesame seeds. Cut each pita into 6 wedges. Arrange the wedges in a single layer on a baking sheet. Bake until lightly brown, about 8 minutes. Transfer to a rack and let cool.

The chips can be stored in an airtight container at room temperature for 2 weeks.

Yogurt Cheese

Makes 1½ cups (360 mL)

3 cups	plain yogurt	720 mL

Line a colander or a strainer with a coffee filter or cheesecloth. Place over a medium bowl. Spoon the yogurt into the strainer and cover with plastic wrap. Let sit at least 4 hours or up to 24 hours in the refrigerator. Remove the yogurt cheese from the strainer and discard the liquid from the bowl.

Yogurt cheese can be stored in an airtight container in the refrigerator for 2 weeks.

Middle Eastern and Indian cooks have been using yogurt cheese for centuries in their cooking. Look for a natural yogurt that contains no gelatin. Replace mayonnaise and cream cheese in your dips with low-fat yogurt cheese.

 # Crème Fraîche

Makes 2 cups (475 mL)

2 cups	whipping cream	475 mL
2 Tbsp.	buttermilk	30 mL

In a small saucepan, heat the cream over low heat to barely warm. Place in a jar with a tight-fitting lid. Add the buttermilk and shake well. Cover and let stand at room temperature for 12–24 hours. The mixture will become thick and creamy. Refrigerate for 24 hours before using.

Crème fraîche can be stored in an airtight container in the refrigerator for 2 weeks. Save 1 Tbsp. (15 mL) to replace the buttermilk in your next batch.

Crème fraîche is a rich, high-fat cultured cream used in French cooking to thicken soups and sauces or to replace whipping cream in desserts. It is worth the small effort required to make it.

Pesto

Makes 1/2 cup (120 mL)

2	cloves garlic	2
1/4 cup	pine nuts, toasted	60 mL
2 cups	fresh basil leaves, packed	475 mL
1 tsp.	fresh lemon juice	5 mL
1/3 cup	olive oil	80 mL
1/4 cup	freshly grated Parmesan cheese	60 mL

In a food processor or blender, chop the garlic and pine nuts. Add the basil and lemon juice and pulse until chunky. With the motor running, add the oil in a slow stream, until a creamy paste forms. Scrape down the sides of the food processor. Add the Parmesan cheese and pulse 5 seconds longer. The pesto can be stored in an airtight container in the refrigerator for 2 days or frozen for 6 months.

The name "pesto" comes from the Italian verb *pestare*, to use a mortar and pestle, and traditionally is made using fresh sweet basil. Modern cooks use a food processor or blender, and basil can be replaced with fresh cilantro, parsley, arugula or mint. The sauce can be frozen in an ice-cube tray, transferred to a plastic bag and kept frozen for up to 6 months. It's a great addition to creamy dips, sauces and soups.

Fresh Tomato Sauce

Makes approximately 1¹/₂ cups (360 mL)

2 Tbsp.	olive oil	30 mL
1	onion, chopped	1
4	cloves garlic, minced	4
1	28-oz. (796-mL) can diced plum tomatoes	1
1 Tbsp.	chopped fresh basil, or ¹/₂ tsp. (2.5 mL) dried	15 mL
¹/₄ tsp.	salt	1.2 mL
¹/₈ tsp.	freshly ground black pepper	.5 mL

This is a delicious and flavorful tomato sauce with lots of garlic. If you prefer a milder sauce, decrease the garlic and add more basil.

Heat the oil in a large non-stick saucepan. Add the onion and garlic and cook over medium heat until tender. Add the canned tomatoes and basil. Bring to a boil and cook, uncovered, for 10 minutes. Lower the heat and cook for 15 minutes longer, or until the sauce is thick. Season with salt and pepper.

The sauce can be stored in an airtight container in the refrigerator for 5 days.

Index

About the Author

Marisa Curatolo's cooking career began early. As a child, she
spent hours in the kitchens of her mother and grandmother,
experiences which nurtured a love for food and cooking.
Marisa has trained at École le Notre in Paris and the Dubrulle
French Culinary School in Vancouver. She now owns The
Cooking Studio, a Winnipeg cooking school, as well as a
private dining room. She lives in Winnipeg, Manitoba, with her
husband and two young sons.